THE DEVELOPMENT OF MILTON'S PROSE STYLE

THOMAS N. CORNS

CLARENDON PRESS OXFORD
1982

Oxford University Press, Walton Street, Oxford OX2 6DP
London Glasgow New York Toronto
Delhi Bombay Calcutta Madras Karachi
Kuala Lumpur Singapore Hong Kong Tokyo
Nairobi Dar es Salaam Cape Town
Melbourne Auckland
and associate companies in
Beirut Berlin Ibadan Mexico City

Published in the United States by
Oxford University Press, New York

British Library Cataloguing in Publication Data
Corns, Thomas N.
The development of Milton's prose style
(Oxford English monographs)
1. Milton, John, 1608-1674 — Prose I. Title
828'.408   PR3581
ISBN 0-19-811717-5

Library of Congress Cataloging in Publication Data
Corns, Thomas N.
The development of Milton's prose style.
(Oxford English monographs)
Bibliography: p.
Includes index.
1. Milton, John, 1608-1674 — Style. 2. Milton, John, 1608-1674 — Prose. I. Title.
PR3594.C6   821'.4   81-16884
ISBN 0-19-811717-5   AACR2

Typeset and printed in Great Britain by
The Thetford Press Limited, Thetford, Norfolk

To
Robert
and
Richard

ACKNOWLEDGEMENTS

This study began as a doctoral dissertation presented to the University of Oxford. I should like to acknowledge my debt to my supervisors, Professor John Carey and Mr C. J. E. Ball, and to my examiner, Mr Dennis Burden, who made a number of useful suggestions. The first draft of the book was read by Professor A. D. S. Fowler and Dr H. P. Sucksmith, who saved me from several mistakes. Professor Norman Davis, who read the typescript for Oxford English Monographs, kindly pointed out errors and infelicities. Dr J. A. Downie made many encouraging suggestions.

I am indebted to the staffs of the Bodleian Library, the British Library, and the Library of the University College of North Wales, the Oxford University Computing Laboratory, the University of Manchester Regional Computing Centre, and the University College of North Wales Computing Laboratory.

My wife typed various drafts, checked references, confirmed calculations, and provided much practical help and support.

Bangor,   T.N.C.
July 1981

CONTENTS

Introduction   xi

List of Short Titles   xiii

SECTION I: THE ANTI-PRELATICAL TRACTS (1641 to 1642) AND THE FINAL PAMPHLETS (1659 to 1673)

1.	Word Frequencies	1
2.	Other Lexical Features	6
3.	Syntactical Features excluding Sentence Structure	20
4.	Sentence Structure	31
5.	Imagery	43
6.	Conclusions to Section I	64

SECTION II. THE TRACTS OF 1643 to 1645 AND 1649

7.	Word Frequencies	66
8.	Other Lexical Features	69
9.	Syntax	80
10.	Imagery	83
11.	Conclusions	101

Appendix   104

Notes   106

Bibliography   112

Index   117

INTRODUCTION

This study originates in the belief that previous accounts of Milton's prose neither identify what is really unique to him nor adequately describe how his style changes.

Milton's prose should be considered against contemporary stylistic norms for the same genre. Our appreciation of his style has been distorted through concentration on those features which merely distinguish him from writers who were not his contemporaries or who were producing a different kind of literature.

Linguists have observed how style changes with situation.[1] It is patently the case that nowadays the stylistic norms of a newspaper editorial differ from those of the sports-page, those of an academic discourse differ from those of a political treatise, even that those of a lecture differ from those of an essay, albeit an essay on the same subject. Similar sorts of stylistic marking certainly operated at most earlier stages of the English language. Moreover, the norms for each category have changed diachronically with the language. For example, stylistic norms for the twentieth-century political treatise differ from those of the Victorian equivalent as well as from those of the modern academic discourse.

It is misleading, then, to compare Milton with Hooker or Browne, as Hamilton[2] and Stavely[3] have done, in that the former is not a contemporary and neither, strictly, is writing political pamphlets. Again, Emma's procedure of isolating those features which distinguish Milton from T. S. Eliot and Shakespeare has little to recomment it.[4] Stavely also compares Milton with Leveller propagandists. This appears more promising, but still may be misleading. In the context of the whole range of Civil War pamphleteering the style of the Levellers may well be eccentric. Where they differ from Milton, it is just as likely to be their style, not Milton's, that is out of step.

I have designed my study as an essay in historical stylistics. I compare each group of Miltonic tracts with pamphlets by other writers contributing to the same controversies that concerned Milton and representing as wide a range of political and ideological positions as feasible.[5] I have attempted to reconstruct the genre expectations of Milton's first readers, so that, without surrendering the critical and analytical positions of the twentieth century, we may rediscover some of the genuine freshness and innovation which his original audience would have appreciated. In the process, many of those elements which seem so extraordinary to the uninformed modern reader and which, indeed, have preoccupied the modern critic, fade to unimportance, recognized as merely commonplace in that genre at that time.

All references to Milton's prose are to the Yale edition, except for *Of True Religion*. References to this text are to the otherwise superseded Columbia edition.

Line numbers are given where references are made to single words extracted from their contexts.

The following abbreviations are used:

MP   *Modern Philology*
PMLA   *Proceedings of the Modern Language Association of America*
PQ   *Philological Quarterly.*

LIST OF SHORT TITLES

i. Works by Milton

Columbia	*The Works of John Milton*, ed. Frank Allen Patterson *et al.* (New York, 1931-8).
Yale	*Complete Prose Works of John Milton*, ed. Don M. Wolfe *et al.* (New Haven, 1953-).
Poems	*The Poems of John Milton*, ed. John Carey and Alastair Fowler (1968).
Of Reformation	*Of Reformation touching Church-Discipline in England* (1641).
Prelatical Episcopacy	*Of Prelatical Episcopacy* (1641).
Animadversions	*Animadversions upon the Remonstrants Defence against Smectymnuus* (1641).
Church-Government	*The Reason of Church-Government Urg'd against Prelaty* (1642).
Apology	*An Apology against a Pamphlet Call'd A Modest Confutation* (1642).
Doctrine	*The Doctrine and Discipline of Divorce* (1643, 1644).
Of Education	*Of Education. To Master Samuel Hartlib* (1644).
Areopagitica	*Areopagitica; A Speech for the Liberty of Unlicens'd Printing* (1644).
Tetrachordon	*Tetrachordon: Expositions upon the Four Chief Places in Scripture which Treat of Marriage* (1645).
Colasterion	*Colasterion: A Reply to a Nameless Answer Against the Doctrine and Discipline of Divorce* (1645).
Tenure	*The Tenure of Kings and Magistrates* (1649).
Observations	*Observations upon the Articles of Peace with the Irish Rebels* (1649).
Eikonoklastes	*Eikonoklastes: in Answer to a Book Intitl'd Eikon Basilike* (1649).
Civil Power	*A Treatise of Civil Power in Ecclesiastical Causes* (1659).
Hirelings	*Considerations touching the Likeliest Means to Remove Hirelings out of the Church* (1659).
Brief Notes	*Brief Notes upon a Late Sermon, Titl'd, The Fear of God and the King* (1660).

Readie and Easie Way	*The Readie and Easie Way to Establish a Free Commonwealth* (1660).
Of True Religion	*Of True Religion, Heresy, Schism, and Toleration* (1673).

ii. Other Works

Humble Remonstrance	Joseph Hall, *An Humble Remonstrance to the High Court of Parliament* (1640).
Defence of Humble Remonstrance	——, *A Defence of the Humble Remstrance* (1641).
Short Answer	——, *A Short Answer to the Tedious Vindication of Smectymnuus* (1641).
Answer to Humble Remonstrance	Smectymnuus, *An Answer to a Book Entitled, an Humble Remonstrance* (1641).
Vindication of Answer	——, *A Vindication of the Answer to the Humble Remonstrance* (1641).
Modest Confutation	*A Modest Confutation of a Slanderous and Scurrilous Libell, Entituled, Animadversions* (1642).
Mans Mortallitie	R. O., *Mans Mortallitie* (Amsterdam, 1643).
Answer to a Book	Anon., *An Answer to a Book, Intituled, The Doctrine and Discipline of Divorce* (1644).
Bloudy Tenent	Roger Williams, *The Bloudy Tenent of Persecution for cause of Conscience* (1644).
Dippers Dipt	Daniel Featley, *The Dippers Dipt* (1645).
Eikon Basilike	Charles I, *Eikon Basilike* (1649).
Eikon Alethine	Anon., *Eikon Alethine* (1649).
Golden Rule	John Canne, *The Golden Rule, Or, Justice Advanced* (1649).
Humble Address	Henry Hammond, *To the Right Honourable, the Lord Fairfax, and His Councell of Warre: The Humble Address* (1649).
Interest	Marchemont Nedham, *Interest Will Not Lie* (1659).
Brief Necessary Vindication	William Prynne, *A Brief Necessary Vindication of the Old and New Secluded Members* (1659).
Good Old Cause	Henry Stubbe, *An Essay in Defence of the Good Old Cause* (1659).
Dignity of Kingship	G.S., *The Dignity of Kingship Asserted* (1660).

Section I: The Anti-prelatical Tracts (1641 to 1642) and the Final Pamphlets (1659 to 1673)

1. WORD FREQUENCIES

A basic distinction[1] is observed throughout this chapter between words as units of speech or writing, that is, as the series of sound or visual symbols that constitute the smallest independent units of meaning, and lexical words, that is, different items of vocabulary. A printed page may consist of perhaps three hundred words in the former sense, but perhaps only one hundred *different* lexical words. 'Word frequency' is the frequency of lexical words within the samples of printed or spoken words.

The investigation of this aspect of style is based on the computer analysis of 3,000-word samples taken from the beginning of every Miltonic tract and each of the contemporary pamphlets selected for comparison. I normalized the spelling of the texts for computer processing. Sample size was determined by the length of the shortest tracts (about 3,000 words). Such samples constitute about ten of the smallish quarto pages in which most of the pamphlets were originally published, and it seemed reasonable to me that the distinctions in this aspect of style, if indeed important, would probably be apparent from passages of this length. I made no attempt at lemmatization.[2]

Table 1 shows the number of lexical words that occur once and the total number of lexical words within the samples from the first and last Miltonic groups and the tracts selected for comparison with them.

Milton in the samples from his anti-prelatical tracts uses more lexical items than in all but the second edition of *Readie and Easie Way*, though the first edition comes close to penetrating the range of his first tracts. Again, but for the second edition of *Readie and Easie Way*, the samples from his first pamphlets have

TABLE 1

Word frequencies in samples from first and final groups

	lexical words occurring once	total vocabulary
Miltonic: first group		
Of Reformation	857	1,141
Prelatical Episcopacy	663	971
Animadversions	855	1,151
Church-Government	763	1,045
Apology	682	980
Miltonic: final group		
Civil Power	493	826
Hirelings	514	873
Readie and Easie Way (1st edn.)	656	962
Readie and Easie Way (2nd edn.)	714	1,025
Brief Notes	616	926
Of True Religion	625	941
Non-Miltonic: first group		
Humble Remonstrance	692	1,013
Defence of Humble Remonstrance	637	953
Short Answer	654	964
Answer to Humble Remonstrance	540	880
Vindication of Answer	642	955
Modest Confutation	698	992
Non-Miltonic: final group		
Dignity of Kingship	663	1,011
Brief Necessary Vindication	571	910
Interest	614	943
Good Old Cause	620	918

more words occurring once than any of his last tracts. The first edition of *Readie and Easie Way* has almost as many singletons as *Prelatical Episcopacy*. There is no evidence to suggest that this trend merely reflects a development in the genre as a whole over the period of the Civil War and Interregnum. In general, it would seem, Milton in his early tracts uses more lexical items than most contemporaries. None approaches *Animadversions* or *Of Reformation* and only three pamphlets—the *Humble Remonstrance*, the *Modest Confutation*, and, from the later group, *The Dignity of Kingship Asserted*—exceed what are, in this respect, his most limited anti-prelactical tracts. In contrast, the final Miltonic tracts, with the exception of the two editions of *Readie and Easie Way*, have a more restricted number of lexical items than all but three of the non-Miltonic pamphlets from either period.

Several hypotheses suggest themselves. Word frequency is not independent of content. A passage in which an allusion is made to many concepts may well draw upon a wider vocabulary than one in which an author considers a restricted subject in greater depth. Again, a passage that contains a lot of imagery may have more lexical items because concepts outside the central area of reference are introduced through analogy. The distinct alteration in Milton's word frequency may seem explicable simply in terms of changes in his dialectic or use of imagery. However, close scrutiny of his use of vocabulary inclines me to believe that, though these other factors cannot be completely discounted, the changing pattern of word frequency reflects a more radical alteration in the fabric of his prose and in his use of language.

In the final tracts Milton has a distinct preference for using the same words or group of words for each notion alluded to. Thus, in *Civil Power*, within the 3,000-word sample 'scripture' and 'scriptures' together occur 25 times. The only other word used for holy writ is 'gospel' (VII, 245. 14, 245. 18, 249. 24), and that to distinguish the New Testament. 'Conscience', 'consciences', and 'conscientious' occur 24 times and 'religion' and 'religious' 28 times. Milton introduces no synonyms for them. In the sample from *Hirelings* 'hire' and 'hirelings' occur together 20 times, though he occasionally speaks of 'monie' (VII, 279. 7, 279. 10, 280. 10, 283. 24 (twice)), 'gain' (pp. 275. 14, 280. 3), and 'recompense' (p. 279. 12). 'Tithe' and 'tithes' occur 25 times. In *Brief Notes* 'King', 'Kings', and 'Kingship' are used 52 times. The only synonyms are 'monarchie' (VII, 481. 18) and in the perhaps pleonastic phrase 'to be a King or Monarch' (p. 473). These are particularly striking examples, but the proclivity towards using the same words for recurrent concepts also manifests itself in other, smaller clusters.

In contrast, Milton's anti-prelatical tracts are characterized by the use of sets of synonyms. Thus, abuse from Joseph Hall and the apologists of prelacy is variously termed 'dishonest words' (*Apology*, I, 870), 'slanderous bolts' (ibid.), 'libellous endorsements' (ibid.), 'slander' (ibid., 1. 28), 'sharpe taunts' (p. 872), 'frumps and curtall gibes' (p. 873), and 'reproaches and reviles' (p. 875). Again, in *Prelatical Episcopacy*, the works of the Church Fathers are represented as 'stale, and uselesse records of either uncertaine, or unsound antiquity' (I, 624) and 'gay testimonies' (p. 627). Ignatius presents 'a doubtfull relation' (p. 628), Polycrates a 'legendarie piece' (p. 633) or 'traditionall ware' (p. 634). The epistles of Ignatius are variously 'a supposititious ofspring' (p. 635), 'spurious' (ibid., 1. 12), 'interlarded with Corruptions' (p. 637), and 'adulterat' (p. 639. 1). In the course of the pamphlet, in neat contrast with the very restricted cluster from *Civil Power* considered above, Milton uses not only the recurrent terms 'Bible', 'Gospel', and 'Scriptures', but draws also a range of alternatives, 'holy writ' (p. 627), 'that sovran book' (p. 631), 'the pure Evangelick Manna' (p. 639), 'holy Text' (p. 651), and '*Gods* word' (p. 652).

The practice of drawing on such lexical sets radically distinguishes the texture of the earliest texts from the last. The following typifies his anti-prelatical pamphlets:

The first and greatest reason of Church-government, we may securely with assent of many on the adverse part, affirme to be, because we finde it so ordain'd and set out to us by the appointment of God in the Scriptures; but whether this be Presbyteriall, or Prelaticall, it cannot be brought to the scanning, untill I have said what is meet to some who do not think it for the ease of their inconsequent opinions, to grant that Church discipline is platform'd in the Bible, but that it is left to the discretion of men (*Church-Government*, I, 750).

Milton avoids reptition of words. Hence, 'discipline' for 'government', 'platform'd' for 'set out', and 'the Scriptures' for 'the Bible'. Compare with this:

But if any man shall pretend, that the Scripture judges to his conscience for other men, he makes himself greater not only then the church, but also then the scripture, then the consciences of other men . . . (*Civil Power*, VII, 247).

Here he reiterates the same words, even the same phrases, in a manner alien to the general style of his first tracts.

Of course, examples can be found in the last pamphlets where Milton utilizes synonyms to avoid repetition, as in the group 'is taxt', 'is secured', 'are charged' in *Of True Religion* (Columbia,

VI, 169). On the whole, however, the distinction holds good. *Readie and Easie Way* presents the major exception. The first edition has more lexical items than any among the final tracts. the second marks a full-blooded return to the practice of his earlier style. Thus, for example, for some of the recurrent concepts he generates such groups as 'bondage' (VII, 407. 9), 'Servitude' (p. 408. 10), 'tyrannie' (p. 409.19), 'thraldom' (p. 410. 2), 'slaverie' (p. 422. 19), and 'subjection' (p. 426. 8), which bring a number of emotionally-charged alternatives to bear on his target.

2. OTHER LEXICAL FEATURES[1]

In order to establish, albeit very roughly indeed, the extent to which Milton and contemporary pamphleteers utilize words new to the language, I attempted to identify words not recorded before 1600 by the *OED*. Obviously, not every word could be checked and some judgement had to be exercised about which words were worth looking up. Though these amounted to several thousands, no doubt I have missed more than a few. The word lists thus derived pose serious interpretative problems. I noted considerably more examples in Milton's earlier tracts than in his last ones. If only words that occur within forty years or so of publication are noted (that is, if 1620 is regarded as the earliest date at which words in the last tracts are considered neologisms), then the distinction between the periods is even sharper. However, in general the earlier tracts are much longer and even if we could be sure—as we cannot—that the lists were exhaustive, comparison between findings from such disparate linguistic universes would be hazardous since we should not be comparing like with like. The lists from the two non-Miltonic groups present similar difficulties in interpretation. The only sure conclusion is that at neither period do Milton and his contemporaries show reluctance about using neologisms.

More interesting is the sort of recently coined words used. The overwhelming majority of new words used by Milton in both periods are formed from the established resources of the language, either by compounding—'over-dated' (*Of Reformation*, I, 519. 17), 'well-tasted' (*Prelatical Espiscopacy*, I. 629. 10), 'all-knowing' (*Animadversion*, I, 665. 8), 'after game' (*Readie and Easie Way*, VII, 424. 2);[2] or by other kinds of word formation—'disinabling' (*of Reformation*, I, 533. 10), 'uningenuous' (*Hirelings*, VII, 315. 11). Similarly, most neologisms in the non-Miltonic tracts have their origins in the established vocabulary of English and are again formed either through compounding—'Lay-presbytery' (*Defence of Humble Remonstrance*, p. 140. 6), 'Grammar-learning' (*Short Answer*, p. 51.21), 'Journal-Book' (*Interest*, p. 31. 30); or through other kinds of word-formation—'non-preaching' (*Answer to Humble Remonstrance*, p. 12. 26), 'Jesuitism' (*Brief Necessary*

Vindication, p. 43. 6), 'spontaneously' (*Dignity of Kingship*, p. 47. 18). These lists, of course, are illustrative rather than exhaustive.

In both Milton and the others there are plenty of words first noted since 1600 that have their origins outside the native resources of English. Most had entered before 1620, and if the criterion of noting nothing that had entered more than about forty years before publication is applied, numbers from the later tracts of Milton and the others are much depleted. This, no doubt, reflects a further deceleration in the rate of borrowing from the high summer of language expansion in the sixteenth century. In Milton, some of the loan-words are neutral or technical terms—'*homogeneall*' (*Of Reformation*, I. 599. 8), 'Lexicon' (*Prelatical Episcopacy*, I, 632. 7), 'commentitious' (ibid., p. 650. 19). However, in the earlier tracts new and perhaps unassimilated words sometimes, it seems, carry a moral weight by connoting the foreignness, the un-English qualities, of that to which they refer. Consider the following passage:

. . . after all your Monkish prohibitions, and expurgatorious indexes, your gags and snaffles, your proud *Imprimaturs* not to be obtain'd without the shallow surview, but not shallow hand of some mercenary, narrow Soul'd, and illiterate Chaplain . . . (*Animadversions*, I, 669),

'*Imprimaturs*' is conspicuous by its unfamiliarity in English discourse (the first use recorded by the *OED* is from 1640) and it is immediately recognizable as an inflected form of a Latin verb.[3] As used by Milton in the context of this vituperative passage, its strangeness seems to connote the outlandishness of the prelatical censors. The effect is reinforced by the six-syllabled 'expurgatorious', formed by Milton himself from a Latin loan-word, 'expurgate', first noted by the *OED* in 1621, or else directly from the modern Latin 'expurgatorius'. Not only is it unfamiliar and strikingly long, but also its echo of 'purgatory' makes a subtle, perhaps even subliminal connection between the prelates and the Catholicism with which he would associate them. Again, in reply to Joseph Hall's query whether bishops should be allowed to offer hospitality, Milton retorts, 'Bacchanalia's good store in every Bishop's family, and good gleeking' (*Animadversions*, I, 731). Here the word 'Bacchanalia', again unusually long, recently borrowed (first noted in 1633 by the *OED*), and with an un-English termination, suggests the incongruity of lavish living and Mediterranean indulgence for English churchmen. The prelates are rivalling (ancient) Rome in their decadence.

With one or two exceptions, the neologisms of foreign origin employed by the other writers are used simply as technical or neutral terms, without the moral implications the early Milton attaches to some of those he adopts. When 'G.S.', discussing the Dutch republic, says, '. . . the measure of *merit* among them is only *Money* which without either wit, or honesty, or any *Good quality*, shall preferre a sordid *Boorish Churle*, to be one of their *Hoghen Moghen* Heers . . .' (*Dignity of Kingship*, p. 117), then arguably the comic clumsiness of the term 'Hoghen Moghen' (first noted in English in 1638 by the *OED*) and the foreignness of 'Heers' (the *OED* records only the form 'Mynheer', from 1652) suggest something of the outlandish rudeness he would associate with the Dutch. Elsewhere, however, alien-looking words, still retaining their classical inflections, such as 'Theta' (*Answer to Humble Remonstrance*, p. 15. 25), 'Chorepiscopi' (*Defence of Humble Remonstrance*, p. 72, sig. Llv. 19), and '*Prolegomena*' (*Interest*, p. 33. 36), are used quite neutrally and without any attempt to achieve the sort of effect Milton sometimes secured in his anti-prelatical pamphlets.

Milton and the other writers of both periods use plenty of words in significations that apparently developed within the seventeenth century. If only significations noted after 1620 are considered, the lists from all later tracts remain substantial. Particularly conspicuous, especially in the later tracts, are terms that acquired a precise political sense after the inception of open conflict with king and bishops, such as 'decimal' (*OED* 2, *Hirelings*, VII, 312. 23), 'fanatic' (*OED* 2, *Readie and Easie Way*, VII, 453. 1), 'Cavalier' (*OED* 3, ibid., p. 454. 3); and from the non-Miltonic texts (which, of course, contain some of the above) 'Protector' (*OED* 2b, *Interest*, p. 15. 15), 'dismembered' (*OED* 4, *Dignity of Kingship*, p. 3. 19). A distinctive vocabulary for political analysis—and abuse—seems to have developed over the period of the Civil War and Interregnum.

Milton's own coinings which I have identified from the early period outnumber those of the last tracts by roughly three to one.[4] Again, this may merely reflect disparities in pamphlet length. Most are formed from the native resources of English by

the usual kinds of word-formation. Verbs are adopted as nouns
—'petty-fog' (*Prelatical Episcopacy*, I, 648. 5), 'struggl' (*Church-Government*, I, 795. 24); and nouns as verbs—'fescu'd'
(*Animadversions*, I, 682. 16), 'quarterniond' (*Church-Government*,
I, 752. 3). Words are formed by suffixation—'*Aphorismers*' (*Of
Reformation*, I, 598. 23), 'punctualist' (*Church-Government*, I, 825.
9), 'swainish' (*Apology*, I, 890. 8), 'protestantly' (*Civil Power*,
VII, 251. 35), 'reformedly' (*Hirelings*, VII, 294. 17); and by
prefixation—'*Pseudepiscopacy*' (*Animadversions*, I, 662. 21),
'unchasten'd' (*Church-Government*, I, 854. 17), 'unimplicit' (*Of
True Religion*, Columbia, VI, 178. 18). At both stages of his
career Milton does not hesitate to form a new word using the
normal resources of the language if the alternative is some wordy
periphrasis—'makers of aphorisms', 'in a reformed manner',
etc. In his anti-prelatical tracts, some of the words thus generated show a lexical playfulness. For example, 'anticreator'
(*Apology*, I, 880. 22) is coined as part of an elaborate gibe at
Joseph Hall's *Mundus alter et idem* (London, 1605?). Milton
largely through his new coining suggests that Hall, in inventing
the fanciful universe of his satire, is like the Manichaean force of
evil, parodying the creation. Again, 'disgospelling' in 'a cruell
disgospelling jurisdiction' (ibid., p. 952) strikes the more forcefully in that it is the negation, indeed, the reversal, of a verb one
would have thought incapable of being reversed.

The largest and most interesting group of words coined by
Milton from native resources are those he forms by compounding. They constitute roughly as large a share of his coinings in
the late as in the early period. Nearly all his compounds belong
to the endocentric type (that is, each compound has the same
grammatical distribution as one of its elements). I note only one
example of the exocentric structure (that is, one in which neither
element can replace the compound)—'slip-skin' in 'a pretty slip-
skin conveyance' (*Animadversions*, I, 687). Milton's zeal for compounding leads him once to generate, in the phrase 'demeanes
himselfe in the dull expression so like a dough kneaded thing'
(*Apology*, I, 910), a word to which I can think of no structural
analogy[5]—it clearly means 'kneaded as dough is kneaded'.

The majority of Milton's compounds are unremarkable,
reflecting perhaps the same interest in avoiding periphrases as
his previously considered coinings—'Church-history' (*Prelatical*

Episcopacy, I, 630. 11), 'eye-brightning' (*Church-Government*, I, 803. 5), 'state-pensioners' (*Hirelings*, VII, 308. 24), instead of 'history of the Church', 'for brightening the eye', and 'pensioners of the state'. However, a considerable number, all but a few of them in the earlier tracts, show a lexical brilliance of a higher order. Milton compounds words that are not generally juxtaposed, sometimes thus forming, in effect, vivid syncopated images. The connection of 'plurality' with 'gaping' in 'nonresident and plurality-gaping Prelats' (*Apology*, I, 932) equates benefices with comestibles to be mawed down by the greedy bishops. 'Church-maskers' (*Church-Government*, I, 828, 9) and 'Sermon-actor' (*Apology*, I, 935. 17), both applied to the bishops and their supporters, suggest in abbreviated form imagery pointing up the false and histrionic nature of his enemies, as does the epithet 'Pulpit-Mountibank' (*Brief Notes*, VII, 470. 3), which he coins for Dr Griffith, whose sermon he is there attacking. Occasionally, Milton combines more than two elements into fantastic compounds, literary grotesques, which connote the swollen absurdity of those he would attack, as in 'only-Canonwise Prelat' (*Of Reformation*, I, 547) or the much-quoted: '. . . what a plump endowment to the many-benefice-gaping mouth of a Prelate, what a relish it would give to his canary-sucking, and swan-eating palat . . .' (ibid., p. 549). This sort of compounding does not occur in his last tracts at all.

Words formed or borrowed from foreign languages constitute a larger proportion of Miltonic coinings in the early than the late tracts. Occasionally, they are formed to meet the need for a technical term or for a word to name a foreign concept, like '*Salutatory*' (ibid., p. 607. 9), 'Paneguries' (*Animadversions*, I. 820. 1), or 'Tripersonality' (*Of True Religion*, Columbia, VI, 169. 12). However, in the anti-prelatical tracts Milton generally uses them in reference to people or practices he regards with suspicion or contempt in order to indicate their alien character. Thus, he forms from the Greek the word 'Hecatontomes' (*Animadversions*, I, 731. 21) to refer to the series of volumes produced by prelatical writers in refutation of Catholicism. The ink-horn opacity of the word underscores the ink-horn nature of their work, sophisticated but sterile literary efforts when what was needed, in Milton's view, was an active, preaching ministry committed to the implementation of the Gospel. In 'What can be gather'd hence but that the Prelat would still sacrifice? conceave him readers, he would missificate' (*Church-Government*, I, 771), the word 'missificate', taken by Milton from late Latin, communicates the un-English, indeed, thoroughly monkish, flavour of the rites the bishops would perform. '*Madamoisellaes*' and 'Trinculo's' (from the Italianate name of the drunken jester in *The Tempest*) combine interestingly in:

. . . young Divines, and those in next aptitude to Divinity have bin seene so oft upon the Stage writhing and unboning their Clergy limmes to all the antick and dishonest gestures of Trinculo's, Buffoons, and Bawds . . . to the eyes of Courtiers, and Court-Ladies, with their Groomes and *Madamoisellaes*' (*Apology*, I, 887).

The foreignness of Milton's coinings, emphasized by the orthographical difficulty in forming their plurals, suggests that the young clergymen and novices are contaminated with a sinisterly alien decadence.[6]

Non-Miltonic coinings are altogether duller. Word-formation from the native resources of English generally seems less frequent than in Milton, pointing, I feel, to his greater readiness to fashion new words rather than paraphrase. But, of course, his contemporaries do form some new words. Thus, affixation produces, for example, 'mistransported' (*Humble Remonstrance*, p. 11.21), 'irrelievable' (*Good Old Cause*, p. 8. 28), 'sparklingly' (*Dignity of Kingship*, Epistle Dedicatory, sig. A3v. 6). Compounding is usually limited to linking object or attributive nouns to other nouns or to verbal nouns, as in 'Church-Liturgie' (*Humble Remonstrance*, p. 13. 13), 'Babie-baptism' (*Good Old Cause*, p. 130. 30), 'State-pleasing' (*Dignity of Kingship*, pp. 141-2). Few new coinings approach the vividness of Milton's syncopated imagery and unexpected combinations. Perhaps one could point to 'G.S.''s 'State-Jugler' (ibid., p. 36. 30) or Prynne's '*Army-Saints*' (*Brief Necessary Vindication*, p. 44. 3). Words are very rarely borrowed directly from foreign languages, and these are generally unassimilated technical terms, not noted by the *OED*, as in 'The antiquity of Chancellors, which were the same with *Ecclesiecdici*, or *Episcoporum ecdici*, (*Defence of Humble Remonstrance*, p. 80). The Smectymnuans produce some bizarre words from foreign material, as in 'then is it [Church-Government] Τωv κακιστωv κρατοs Kakistocraticall' (*Vindication of Answer*, p. 82) or

'. . . let him suffer as an Hieronymomastix, that when Hierome crosses his opinion, calls him a *waspish hot, good man*' (ibid., p. 83), but they seem merely to delight in the abstruseness and specious erudition of such words.

It has been claimed as a major feature of Milton's prose style that he uses Latinate words in such a way that they are reminiscent of their etymological senses.[7] I have found no evidence to indicate that this is really an important element in his usage of words of classical origin. In his first and last tracts I note a handful of genuine examples. For instance, Milton sometimes plays on the word 'schism', as in '*schisme* of a slic't prayer' (*Apology* I, 938)[8] and, as the Yale editor of *Church-Government* notes (I, 786 n. 53), he quibbles quite extensively on the classical sense in that pamphlet. However, it is very easy to overstate how often Milton harks back to earlier, un-English significations of loan-words. For example, the Yale editor of *Church-Government* claims that Milton uses 'decent' in 'the Latin sense of fitting or suitable' (I, 754 n. 26) and again that 'mediocrity' has 'the Latin sense of moderation, temperance' (ibid., p. 856 n. 37). Indeed, these may well be the 'Latin senses', but, as is clear from the *OED*,[9] they are also senses generally current in seventeeth-century English. The editor also asserts that 'preventive' in the phrase 'preventive fear' preserves 'the Latin sense of "going before"' (*Church-Government*, I, 806 n. 34). However, though this is the first time the word (first noted in 1639) is recorded in this signification by the *OED*, the verb 'prevent' was used contemporaneously to mean 'to come, arrive, or appear before'.[10] Milton's usage, then, commits no stunning act of semantic atavism. Loan-words not long assimilated into the language very often retained primary significations which they have since lost. The critic must be alert to the danger of regarding this normal feature of English as a Miltonic eccentricity. I have noted no examples among the non-Miltonic writers of the use of classical loan-words in genuinely un-English significations.

However, I have noted in Milton's anti-prelatical and final tracts over fifty occasions on which he extends a word beyond its established semantic range in other ways. Most such words occur in the first group, but again this may well just reflect their greater length, rather than any important shift in Milton's use of language.

Little critical ingenuity need be expended on many of the words he extends. For example, the substantive 'fume' had for long meant 'odorous smoke (e.g. that of incense, tobacco)'.[11] It is a slight semantic shift for Milton to extend the verb 'fume' to mean 'perfume with incense', as in 'they hallow'd it [dealings with God], they fum'd it, they sprincl'd it' (*Of Reformation*, I, 521). Again, the nouns 'epicure' and 'epicurean' had long since degenerated into denoting, not a follower of Epicurus, but a glutton, a sybarite.[12] We need register no surprise when Milton similarly extends the range of the adjective, as he does in the phrase 'their unctuous, and epicurean paunches' (*Or Reformation*, I, 611).

In a number of cases he uses verbs transitively that had previously been used intransitively—'suffraging' (ibid., p. 600. 11), 'sobs' (*Apology*, I. 908. 8), 'Judaiz'd' (*Hirelings*, VII, 291. 38); and intransitively words that previously were used only transitively—'acuminating' (*Animadversions*, I, 790. 19), 'articulating' (*Apology*, I, 914. 27). These suggest Milton's impatience with the constrictions of linguistic convention—and a tendency to use words as he wished to use them, irrespective of custom.

Some of his semantic extensions in the anti-prelatical tracts are ingenious and exciting. Consider:

. . . they would bear us in hand that we must of duty still appear before them once a year in *Jerusalem* like good circumcizd *males*, and *Females* to the scons't our head money, our tuppences in their Chaunlerly Shop-book of *Easter* (*Of Reformation*, I, 612).

The term 'scons't', according to the *OED*,[13] had previously been applied only to the disciplining of university students. By this widened application Milton suggests that the exaction of the Easter offering reduces the status of the Christian to that of an undergraduate fined by his dean. But the creative use of language does not end there. 'Sconce', the substantive, means 'head', and here it is 'head money' that is being collected 'by the poul'. Milton is being playful. Again , in *Animadversions*, he says that he aims to humble Bishop Hall, '*to send home his haughtinesse well bespurted with his owne holy-water*' (I, 662). Here he fashions a mock title, 'his haughtinesse', in analogy with 'his Highness' or 'his 'Holiness', as if Hall's assured arrogance were a quality characterizing and, indeed, institutionalized in the office he held. He dismisses those who would withhold their sons from church employment if the 'lure and whistle of earthly preferment' were abolished, with: '. . . let not those wretched Fathers thinke they shall impoverish the Church of willing, and able supply, though they keep back their sordid sperm begotten in the lustinesse of their avarice . . .' (ibid., p. 722). 'Sperm', extended to mean 'children', forcefully links the product of procreation with the process of procreation. It communicates Milton's perhaps squeamish revulsion from the raw, bestial carnality of generation by such men.

I found less than a score of semantic extensions among the first and final groups of non-Miltonic tracts. This strongly suggests that Milton felt a greater confidence about shaping the lexis of English to his requirements. All the non-Miltonic examples are stylistically unremarkable.

Critics agree that Milton in his prose draws upon registers of English that his poetry rarely touches, particularly upon the language of colloquial English in general, and slang in particular. Ekfelt, for example, points to what he would identify as 'the coarseness with which he and Hall bespaul each other' in their contributions to the Smectymnuan debate.[14] However, I find it difficult to assess this aspect of an earlier writer's style. The *OED* depends entirely on written records, so it cannot indicate whether a word would more usually appear in spoken English, and in any case, the spoken language of the time was not, of course, directly recorded on any scale or with any accuracy, though we have dictionaries of slang, of the language of 'the canting crew', dating from Milton's period, and these may furnish some limited assistance. However, I have formed the impression that the orthodox view about Milton's use of slang is probably incorrect. Certainly, as Sykes Davies[15] claims, there are some words in Milton's prose which are of colloquial origin and which had only recently established themselves in the written language, such as 'foisted' (*Prelatical Episcopacy*, I, 636. 4), a gamblers' term first noted in 1599, 'trollops' (*Apology*, I, 914. 17), first noted 1615, 'kecking' (ibid., p. 885. 3), 1601, and 'rookd' (*Hirelings*, VII, 297. 30), more gaming slang, noted in 1590. However, it is impossible to be sure of the status of these words by the mid-seventeenth century. As Partridge has observed, slang words can have great social and registral mobility. He cites the example of 'at fault', slang of the hunting field, which, when used figuratively, was assimilated into standard English 'within thirty years'.[16] When Milton adopts a word like 'foisted' or Nedham uses 'turn'd up Trump' (*Interest*, p. 13), they are, I suspect, no more drawing directly on the lexis of gamblers' slang than a modern leader-writer is when he says some politician 'makes his last throw' or 'follows suit'. Moreover, there seems in general to be a critical vagueness about what constitutes a slang or colloquial word or phrase, as distinct from a notion or reference that is rude, unpleasant, or obscene. A critic could make several observations about Milton's rejoinder to Hall and his fellow prelates, 'Wipe your fat corpulencies out of our light' (*Animadversions*, I, 732). It is lexically unusual—note the extension of the normally abstract noun 'corpulency' to denote something concrete, the use of 'light' where one might perhaps have expected 'sight',[17] and the juxtaposition of the plain English 'fat' and 'wipe' with the hard word of Latin origin. Also, it is patently a very impolite remark for a young man to make to a bishop. But it is quite misleading to call it, as Masson does, 'sheer Billingsgate'.[18] Fish-porters do not, I believe, banter each other with four-syllabled Latinate words, nor is any of the words Milton uses in his retort inherently shocking or out of place in written English. Rather, as here, Milton often rudely and aggressively assails social superiors and frequently mentions subjects distasteful to many modern readers and, most probably, to some of his contemporaries also. When he speaks of emesis, venereal disease, and sexual impropriety he does so in general without recourse to euphemism, using words from the core of the language, such as 'spue' (*Readie and Easie Way*, VII, 452. 7), 'Venereal pox' (ibid., p. 453), 'common stales' (*Of Reformation*, I, 531), 'Strumpet' (*Animadversions*, I, 686. 20), etc. When he does use polite circumlocutions, as in 'to accept quietly as a perfume, the over-head emptying of some salt lotion' (ibid., p. 670), he does so to achieve a comic effect.

It is difficult to comment with absolute confidence on the collocations Milton habitually formed. This is, of course, an aspect of lexis that has only quite recently received the systematic attention of linguists, and therefore goes almost unconsidered by the *OED*. The critic must move only tentatively towards con-

clusions about the language of a writer so remote in time from us
as Milton. Pointers come from the examples cited by the *OED*. I
find some evidence to suggest that Milton's lexis, in the anti-
prelatical tracts at least, is characterized by the formation of
abnormal collocations, that is, by the practice of placing words
in close syntactical proximity to classes of words they are not
normally brought into association with. In the most frequent of
these he uses abstract nouns in environments which would normally predict concrete, animate, or human substantives. Thus,
for example, he writes of '*buried Truth*' (*Of Reformation*, I, 526),
though 'buried' seems to collocate usually with concrete nouns.
It is curious to suggest that that which has no physical being can
be interred. 'Adoration' is 'glouting' (ibid., p. 523), again, a
verb usually used of animate nouns. 'Falsehood and Neglect'
had 'throwne' the Bible into dusty corners (ibid., p. 524). He
writes of '*Faith* needing not the weak, and fallible offices of the
Senses' (ibid., pp. 519-20), though normally, I believe, only animate nouns are said to feel or exhibit need. 'Indifference' is a
'persecuter' (*Apology*, I, 925) and 'schisme' a 'bold lurker'
(*Church-Government*, I, 779), words elsewhere used of human
agents. In 'vertue that wavers is not vertue, but vice revolted
from itselfe, and after a while returning' (ibid., p. 795), the
collocations of the abstracts with 'wavers' (a verb rarely noted
before with abstracts) and 'revolted' (it seems from the examples
cited by the *OED* used elsewhere only of humans) makes them
appear concrete and animate. The rhetoric term, 'personification', could appropriately be applied to some examples where
the process is protracted and the environment predicts a human,
rather than merely a concrete, noun, as in:

. . . [Prelaty] againe shall hold such dominion over your captive
minds, as returning with an insatiat greedinesse and force upon your
worldly wealth and power wherewith to deck and magnifie herself, and
her false worships, she shall spoil and havock your estates, disturbe
your ease, diminish your honour, inthraul your liberty . . . (ibid., pp.
850-1).

However, most examples are too abbreviated to be thus accom-
modated, and separating them from the more obtrusive
manifestations of the feature disguises their common origin in
the linguistic phenomenon of abnormal collocation. It is,

rather, a general, persistent tendency in the early tracts to treat abstracts as concrete, animate, and sometimes human, through which Milton represents the great ideals of the Reformation and the elements that threaten them not as intellectual abstractions, but as tangible, living forces in a vital struggle. This is a much less prominent feature of his final group of tracts. We find, for instance 'take our leaves of Libertie' (*Readie and Easie Way*, VII, 409), a phrase which seems normally to have a human object. Examples are much fewer and duller than in his anti-prelatical pamphlets.

In his early tracts words relating to books or style are sometimes placed in environments that would normally predict animate nouns. For example, prelatical propagandists would lead the credulous from 'places of safety under the tuition of holy writ' (*Prelatical Episcopacy*, I, 627). 'Tuition', it seems, generally collocates with a human agent. The prelates 'would have Saint *Pauls* words rampe one over another, as they use to clime into their livings and *Bishopricks*' (*Animadversions*, I, 709). Prose is a 'mortall thing' (*Church-Government*, I, 808), though 'mortall' otherwise collocates with things that have life. Hall resorts to 'snapping adagies' (*Apology*, I, 872). The Smectymnuans lie at the mercy of his 'coy flurting stile' (ibid., p. 873). 'Flurt', I believe, is elsewhere collocated with animate and usually human subjects and 'coy' only with people or behaviour. The North 'lies plunder'd and over-run by a liturgie' (*Animadversions*, I, 732). Critics have noticed that often in the imagery of *Areopagitica* Milton attributes life to books, and have treated this as part of his polemic strategy.[19] However, in the earlier pamphlets it seems a Miltonic habit of thought to consider style and verbal complexes as though they were animate. For him, in this rather unusual way, the style is the man. What people write presents an extension of themselves, something animate and active. The bishops would have words behave as they behave. Hall's style appears much as Milton perceives Hall himself, 'coy' and 'flurting', arch and smugly teasing. I have noted no such collocational abnormalities in his final tracts, though it must be said that there he has little to say about other men's style.

Not all the interesting collocations of the anti-prelatical tracts fall into these two categories. Sometimes enemies are linked to words normally collocated with animals. For example, he writes, 'wee shall see *Antichrist* [i.e. the Pope] shortly wallow heere, though his chiefe Kennell be at *Rome*' (*Of Reformation*, I, 590). He calls the Modest Confuter a 'hip-shot *Grammarian*' (*Apology*, I, 911), a term normally applied to broken-down horses. Other collocations follow no pattern. Consider:

. . . rather let them take heed what lessons they instill into that lump of flesh which they are the cause of, lest, thinking to offer him as a present to God, they dish him out for the Devill (*Animadversions*, I, 722).

It is not immediately apparent that Milton is talking about children. To call a child 'a lump of flesh' is not imagery, for it is literally true, yet the word 'lump' so rarely applies to humans that the effect is dehumanization. Similarly, a father 'begets' or 'engenders' a son: he is not normally 'the cause' of him. 'Dish' as a verb usually collocates with food. Milton's choice of words controls how we respond to the children these fathers would foist on the Church. They are spiritless, just so much meat to be served up. Examples of such lexical innovation abound throughout the early tracts. They are much harder to find in his last ones.

Interesting collocations occur very rarely in the non-Miltonic groups except for a few in the pamphlets of Joseph Hall and in the *Modest Confutation*. Hall has 'your Charity accuseth me' (*Defence of the Humble Remonstrance*, p. 148), an abstract linked with a verb which seems normally to be linked with human subjects. The Modest Confuter talks of 'Envie' as 'make-bate' (*Modest Confutation*, p. 15) and of 'mortified ambition' (ibid., p. 22), again juxtaposing abstracts with terms generally attached to animate nouns. The *Humble Remonstrance* begins with an elaborate personification of the pamphlet:

. . . this honest paper hath broken through the throng, and prostrates it selfe before you: How meanly so ever, and unattended, it presents it selfe to your view, yet it comes to you on a great errand, as the faithfull Messenger of all the peaceable and right-affected sonnes of the Church of *England* . . . (pp. 1-2).

Again, there are one or two words usually used of animals applied to men. Hall will not 'run after the spending of every mouth' (*Defence of the Humble Remonstrance*, p. 3). 'Spending' is a term for the baying of hunting dogs, suggesting that his opponents are ill-trained curs yelping at anything.[20] In the later tracts 'G.S.' claims that apologists for regicide 'bark at *Majesty*' (*Dignity of Kingship*, p. 56) and he suggests that Milton can not act 'without boggling and starting' (ibid., p. 112), terms more appropriate to a badly schooled horse. However, the pervasiveness of unusual, inventive collocations which characterized the early Miltonic tracts and distinguished them from his last pamphlets is nowhere approached.

Many aspects of Milton's lexis in the tracts of 1641 to 1642 exhibit a degree of richness, innovation, wit, and sparkle that sets it apart both from that of his contemporaries and from his own practice in his final tracts.

3. SYNTACTICAL FEATURES EXCLUDING SENTENCE STRUCTURE

Emma in his *Milton's Grammar*[1] attempted to consider Milton's grammatical preferences in poetry and prose within a precise linguistic and quantitative framework. As such his work constituted a refreshing injection of objectivity into a debate which, particularly in connection with Milton's poetry, had become dogmatic and polemical,[2] and his findings point to certain Miltonic syntactical preferences which seem powerfully to serve in distinguishing his style.

However, I have a number of objections to the design of Emma's investigation, and while his findings seem exciting and suggestive the procedure by which he arrived at them remains open to question. (I concerned myself solely with his account of Milton's prose syntax, but most of these objections probably hold good for his other findings.)

His study is based on analysis of 8,000 words from Milton, four 1,000-word samples drawn from major poems, and four samples from his vernacular prose.[3] For comparison he analyses 864 words from Shakespeare (two scenes, *Hamlet*, IV, iv and *The Tempest*, II, ii) and 507 words from T. S. Eliot (from *The Wasteland* and *Burnt Norton*). Emma's samples are too small to command confidence. The 4,000 words from Milton's prose, printed consecutively, would only constitute about thirteen pages of the quarto format in which most of the pamphlets originally appeared. All the non-Miltonic material put together would hardly fill four pages. Yet through these samples Emma presumes to define not only Milton's practice, but also, to some extent, the norms for written English! Clearly, the likelihood of a sample being genuinely representative relates closely to its size: the larger the sample, the less distortive any uncharacteristic or atypical elements it may contain. Again, the authors selected by Emma for comparison with Milton do not satisfy the criteria of situation and contemporaneity. An Elizabethan dramatist and twentieth-century poet are poor choices for comparison with Milton's poetry, but absurd ones for comparison with his prose.

Emma's investigations lead him to formulate a number of statements about Milton's style. It is imperative to know how valid his conclusions are. I have, therefore, largely repeated his inquiry, within the same framework, but, I believe, on a sounder basis, in that works I use for comparison are better selected and my samples are much larger. This chapter is based on the same 3,000-word samples used in the study of word frequencies. The analysis of this corpus into syntactical categories requires the repetition many thousand times of a few simple decisions in classification. At the moment, no computer can effect this chore, since none has a sufficiently large and sophisticated lexicon to distinguish and identify all the words in the texts. However, classification is much easier if there is a concordance to work from, especially if it is printed in the keyword-in-context format, which prints keywords in vertical alignment. Therefore, I created such computer-generated concordances, using a further option of the COCOA package.

The classification of words into parts of speech poses certain taxonomic problems. Emma does not specify by what grammatical system he assigns words to syntactical categories. I opted for the system Milic used in his account of Swift's style, because it is simple and logical and has worked quite well in a similar context.[4]

The first edition of *Readie and Easie Way* scarcely differed in syntactical distribution from the second, to which all findings and references in this chapter relate.

Emma's most interesting conclusions relate to Milton's use of adjectives and verbs. I also believe these to be fertile areas of stylistic investigation, though I do not find Milton's practice as distinctive as Emma does, nor in the ways Emma suggests.

Emma finds that adjectives, including articles

. . . constitute 21.5 per cent of the Milton sample, 23 per cent in the poetry sampled and 21 per cent in the prose. Adjectives make up 15 per cent of the sample of Shakespeare's work and 25 per cent of that of Eliot's. When articles are not included in the count, however, the proportion of adjectives that Milton uses in his poetry . . . exceeds by about three-fourths that found in the sample of Shakespeare and by about one-fifth that in the sample of Eliot (p. 67).

Emma unfortunately omits information about the incidence of adjectives (excluding articles) in Milton's prose. Nevertheless, he uses his figures as a springboard for one of his major critical conclusions, that 'Milton's extensive use of descriptive adjectives may be said to mark him as a poet of qualification more than of predication, one who prefers words that qualify and describe to those that express action' (ibid.). The general implication, though Emma is vague, seems to be that this generalization is applicable also to his prose.[5] My own findings, presented in Table 2, tentatively suggest two conclusions. There

TABLE 2

*Incidence of adjectives in first and final
groups (expressed as percentage of all words in samples)*

	%
Miltonic: first group	
Of Reformation	7.4
Prelatical Episcopacy	6.0
Animadversions	8.5
Church-Government	7.3
Apology	6.9
Miltonic: final group	
Civil Power	5.3
Hirelings	5.2
Readie and Easie Way	7.7
Brief Notes	5.5
Of True Religion	6.5
Non-Miltonic: first group	
Humble Remonstrance	8.3
Defence of Humble Remonstrance	5.5
Short Answer	7.0
Answer to Humble Remonstrance	5.3
Vindication of Answer	5.5
Modest Confutation	5.5
Non-Miltonic: final group	
Dignity of Kingship	7.7
Brief Necessary Vindication	4.4
Interest	6.2
Good Old Cause	4.0

is a change in Milton's practice between the two periods considered here. The incidence of adjectives is marginally higher in the anti-prelatical tracts. The distinction, however, is slight, nor is it consistent. The very late *Of True Religion* penetrates the range of Milton's first pamphlets, and the incidence of adjectives in *Readie and Easie Way*, in a number of other ways an atavistic tract,[6] is higher than the average for the anti-prelatical pamphlets. Nevertheless, it is possible to discern a slight shift in Miltonic practice. Secondly, Emma's conclusion that Milton favours the use of adjectives seems to have some limited validity, though it does not apply in general to the last group. It should further be noted that four tracts (*Humble Remonstrance*, *Short Answer*, *Interest*, and *Dignity of Kingship*) penetrate the range of Milton's anti-prelatical tracts do exhibit a marginally higher practice reflects no distinct trend in the genre. The *average* for the last group of non-Miltonic pamphlets is indeed lower than for the first, but incidence of adjectives in half of them matches that in Milton's first group. In general, it is clear that, though Milton's anti-prelatical tracts do exhibit a margin ally higher than normal incidence of adjectives, there is nothing to support Emma's argument that this is one of the *major* determinants of his style.

More interesting than the crude proportion of adjectives is Milton's changing practice in positioning them with respect to the nouns they qualify. This point does not emerge from Emma's study. He finds that

Of more than 1,600 adjectives in the sample, only 44, or 2.6 per cent, immediately follow the nouns they modify. Of these 44, 40 are in the poetry . . . One can conclude that Milton's customary manner of placing adjectives with respect to their nouns is normal English practice; he did not favour the inversion of normal noun-adjective order and used such inversions mainly in his poetry (p. 69).

In my investigation I altered the scope slightly, counting as postponed any adjective which follows (though not necessarily immediately) the noun to which it refers, but which is not predicated. My findings are presented in Table 3. Clearly, the way in which Milton positions the adjectives he uses is more interesting than Emma suggests. Sporadically in the early period (in *Prelatical Episcopacy* and *Church-Government*) and persistently in later pamphlets Milton uses a decidedly higher proportion of adjectival postponements than all but Stubbe among the contemporaries considered here.

TABLE 3

Positioning of adjectives in first and final
groups (expressed as percentage of all adjectives in samples)

	Before noun %	After noun %	Predi- cated %	Other %
Miltonic: first group				
Of Reformation	83.8	2.3	12.9	0.9
Prelatical Episcopacy	79.1	6.8	12.2	2.0
Animadversions	79.9	1.6	17.0	1.6
Church-Government	72.6	6.6	18.9	1.9
Apology	61.8	2.2	30.2	5.8
Miltonic: final group				
Civil Power	70.9	9.5	14.6	5.1
Hirelings	63.7	7.6	25.5	3.2
Readie and Easie Way	77.8	8.3	11.3	2.6
Brief Notes	64.8	6.8	24.1	4.3
Of True Religion	68.5	8.6	18.8	4.1
Non-Miltonic: first group				
Humble Remonstrance	81.8	5.3	12.9	0
Defence of Humble Remonstrance	76.1	4.9	16.0	3.1
Short Answer	79.3	2.0	14.8	4.0
Answer to Humble Remonstrance	63.2	2.0	25.9	8.8
Vindication of Answer	67.5	5.1	27.4	0
Modest Confutation	68.3	1.9	23.7	6.2
Non-Miltonic: final group				
Dignity of Kingship	80.4	2.5	14.6	2.5
Brief Necessary Vindication	85.2	3.5	7.0	4.2
Interest	82.8	3.2	12.7	1.3
Good Old Cause	71.8	8.2	17.3	2.7

Some of the postponements would support little critical interpretation. Certain adjectives are more usually placed after the
noun they relate to. For example, 'extant', which Milton uses in
'*Eusebius* the ancientest writer extant of Church-history'
(*Prelatical Episcopacy*, I, 630), occurs before the noun it qualifies
in none of the score or so citations before 1864 in the *OED*.

Milton sometimes uses optional inversion purely for aesthetic
effect, as in 'Hire of it self is neither a thing unlawful, nor a word
of any evil note' (*Hirelings*, VII, 279). By inverting 'thing' and
'unlawful' Milton echoes the order of 'word' and its qualifying
phrase 'of evil note', and thus achieves a pleasing and polished
balance.

More usually, however, his inversions serve the interests of clarity and precision. Many fall into two interesting groups, inversions to link the adjective to some phrase which qualifies it and inversions to link the adjective more precisely to the noun to which it refers. Thus, using the former construction he generates phrases like 'many worthy Preachers upright in their lives, powerfull in their audience' (*Church-Government*, I, 754). The inversions permit the adjectives 'upright' and 'powerfull' to be brought into juxtaposition with prepositional phrases defining and limiting their appropriateness. Again, in 'the Protestant religion denies them to be judges, either in themselves infallible or to the consciences of other men' (*Hirelings*, VII, 276), the post-position permits statement of the ways in which men are not infallible judges. Examples could be multiplied, for this is a favourite Miltonic construction, particularly in his final tracts.

In the second postponement structure Milton's objective is to indicate with greater precision the relationship between adjective and noun. Thus, for example, in 'to all due libertie and proportiond equalitie, both human, civil, and Christian' (*Readie and Easie Way*, VII, 424), the postponement allows the group of three adjectives to stand in relation to both 'libertie' and 'equalitie', whereas if it had been placed before 'libertie' not only would the result have been intolerably clumsy ('all due human, civil, and Christian libertie') but also the presence of the words 'all due' before 'libertie' and the participial 'proportiond' applying to 'equalitie' alone may well have suggested that the heavy adjectival group should be taken just with the former noun. Elsewhere, postponement makes it possible for Milton to qualify the link between adjective and noun, as in 'gave to hirelings occasion, though not intended, yet sufficient, to creep at first into the church' (*Hirelings*, VII, 281).

Milton's use of verbs is also noteworthy, but, contrary to Emma's findings, the interest once more lies much less in the crude proportion of verbs than in a finer point of syntactical choice.

Emma finds that verbs constitute 12.8 per cent of the words in his sample from Milton (unfortunately he does not distinguish between poetry and prose), 17.8 per cent of Shakespeare, and 14.6 per cent of Eliot, and he concludes that 'The low frequency of verbs in the sample argues that Milton's preference for the principal qualifying elements of the sentence is maintained partly at the cost of the predicating elements' (p. 86). My own findings are shown in Table 4. Patently there is no evidence to

TABLE 4

Incidence of verbs (including participles,
excluding verbal nouns) in first and final groups
(expressed as percentage of all words in samples)

	%
Miltonic: first group	
Of Reformation	9.9
Prelatical Episcopacy	9.6
Animadversions	10.3
Church-Government	8.3
Apology	10.4
Miltonic: final group	
Civil Power	8.3
Hirelings	8.4
Readie and Easie Way	10.1
Brief Notes	9.6
Of True Religion	9.6
Non-Miltonic: first group	
Humble Remonstrance	9.0
Defence of Humble Remonstrance	10.4
Short Answer	10.9
Answer to Humble Remonstrance	10.7
Vindication of Answer	10.4
Modest Confutation	10.2
Non-Miltonic: final group	
Dignity of Kingship	10.1
Brief Necessary Vindication	9.1
Interest	9.9
Good Old Cause	10.5

support Emma's view that a correlation exists between high incidence of adjectives and low incidence of verbs in the writings of Milton. It should be noted that two of the tracts with the lowest incidence of verbs among the samples analysed, *Civil Power* and *Hirelings*, also have the fewest adjectives among the Miltonic tracts. No clear picture emerges from my investigation. All but three Miltonic tracts fall within the range defined by the practice of his contemporaries. The results are inconclusive and suggest no critical generalization about Milton's practice.

A more interesting aspect of Milton's use of verbs is his enthusiasm for participial constructions.[7] My findings are shown in Table 5. Milton's practice in both groups places him

TABLE 5

Incidence of participles in first and final groups (expressed as percentage of all verbs (including verbal nouns) in samples)

	Present %	Past %	Total %
Miltonic: first group			
Of Reformation	14.1	11.0	25.1
Prelatical Episcopacy	6.8	9.3	16.1
Animadversions	7.4	7.4	14.8
Church-Government	6.4	7.8	14.2
Apology	6.9	6.6	13.5
Miltonic: final group			
Civil Power	10.4	8.9	19.3
Hirelings	8.6	7.5	16.1
Readie and Easie Way	10.0	21.8	31.8
Brief Notes	7.0	12.6	19.6
Of True Religion	4.9	9.1	14.0
Non-Miltonic: first group			
Humble Remonstrance	3.6	8.7	12.3
Defence of Humble Remonstrance	4.7	12.1	16.8
Short Answer	3.1	7.3	10.4
Answer to Humble Remonstrance	5.9	7.0	12.9
Vindication of Answer	7.9	5.6	13.5
Modest Confutation	3.1	5.6	8.7
Non-Miltonic: final group			
Dignity of Kingship	11.0	10.7	21.7
Brief Necessary Vindication	13.6	14.9	28.5
Interest	4.8	5.8	10.6
Good Old Cause	5.7	4.5	10.2

towards the upper end of the range defined by his contemporaries, though it does not distinguish him from four contemporary tracts considered here (*Defence of Humble Remonstrance, Brief Necessary Vindication, Dignity of Kingship,* and *Vindication of Answer*). One Miltonic tract, *Readie and Easie Way,* has more participial constructions than any in either contemporary group. Milton may to some extent have favoured such constructions because they allow him to produce tersely such complex sentences as:

The Parliament of *England*, assisted by a great number of the people who appeered and struck to them faithfullest in defence of religion and thir civil liberties, judging kingship by long experience a government unnecessarie, burdensom and dangerous, justly and magnanimously abolishd it; turning regal bondage into a free Commonwealth, to the admiration and terrour of our emulous neighbours (*Readie and Easie Way*, VII, 409).

The sentence would have been much longer and wordier had Milton expressed subordinate material through relative clauses or other dependent clauses containing finite verbs. However, we must be careful not to overstate how important an element this is in shaping Milton's prose.

The rest of the analysis of syntactical preferences disclosed no further insights into the peculiarities of Milton's prose. In his use of nouns, pronouns, and adverbs he seems solidly in line with the contemporary norms for the genre. Only one further category, conjunctions, merits a fuller discussion, not because Milton's practice is really unusual, but because it has quite erroneously been indentified as the key to Milton's sentence structure.

Emma finds 70 per cent of Milton's conjunctions, in both prose and poetry, are co-ordinating. The proportions for Shakespeare and Eliot are roughly the same. On the basis of this he indulges the following evaluative speculation:

The meaning of the relatively low incidence of subordinating conjunctions, and consequently of subordination, in the poetry of all three men possibly is best explained by observing that co-ordination rather than subordination is the mode of poetry . . . But what is strength for poetry often is weakness in prose . . . as much co-ordination as is suitable to poetry is seldom suited to prose (pp. 129-30).

However, Table 6 shows that Milton's use of co-ordinating conjunctions falls within the range of contemporaries. Furthermore, the structure of Emma's investigation into co-ordination cannot support the sort of interpretation he would make, in that conjunctions often link items other than clauses and sentences. The figures he produces are not really an appropriate basis for comment on sentence structure, though he attempts to relate his findings to the observation of C. E. Vaughan, that 'the style of Milton . . . is in the main not syntactic but paratactic; not a synthesis of clauses, but an agglomeration', which he cites with apparent approval (p. 130 n. 3). Table 7 offers information more

TABLE 6

Incidence of co-ordinating conjunctions in
first and final groups (expressed as percentage of all words
in samples)

	%
Miltonic: first group	
Of Reformation	5.4
Prelatical Episcopacy	4.2
Animadversions	4.2
Church-Government	5.1
Apology	3.7
Miltonic: final group	
Civil Power	3.7
Hirelings	5.0
Readie and Easie Way	5.3
Brief Notes	5.3
Of True Religion	6.8
Non-Miltonic: first group	
Humble Remonstrance	5.9
Defence of Humble Remonstrance	4.1
Short Answer	3.5
Answer to Humble Remonstrance	4.0
Vindication of Answer	6.8
Modest Confutation	3.6
Non-Miltonic: final group	
Dignity of Kingship	5.7
Brief Necessary Vindication	4.9
Interest	4.4
Good Old Cause	5.7

pertinent to the investigation of sentence structure. I have counted those co-ordinating conjunctions that link sentences and clauses (I count participial phrases as clauses), and I have calculated what proportion these constitute of all items (not only co-ordinating and subordinating conjunctions) that link sentences and clauses. It is clear that no facile generalization about high incidence of co-ordination in Milton's prose at clausal and sentence level can be upheld. Milton co-ordinates roughly the same proportion of sentences and clauses as his contemporaries.

TABLE 7

*Incidence of co-ordinating conjunctions in
first and final groups (expressed as percentage of all items
linking clauses and sentences in samples)*

	%
Miltonic: first group	
Of Reformation	35.3
Prelatical Episcopacy	23.5
Animadversions	30.1
Church-Government	26.6
Apology	16.9
Miltonic: final group	
Civil Power	17.2
Hirelings	26.1
Readie and Easie Way	34.4
Brief Notes	27.0
Of True Religion	33.8
Non-Miltonic: first group	
Humble Remonstrance	30.5
Defence of Humble Remonstrance	18.5
Short Answer	22.7
Answer to Humble Remonstrance	25.7
Vindication of Answer	27.0
Modest Confutation	22.2
Non-Miltonic: final group	
Dignity of Kingship	22.6
Brief Necessary Vindication	35.1
Interest	31.0
Good Old Cause	27.8

Patently, the easy paratactic-syntactic dichotomy discloses no
real insights into his sentence structure, and other aspects must
be investigated to isolate the distinguishing qualities of Milton's
practice.

4. SENTENCE STRUCTURE

Emma's study contains a scrutiny of other aspects of Milton's sentence structure, and the area is also investigated at some length by Hamilton[1] and Stavely.[2] Emma adopts a quantitative approach as elsewhere, but analyses fewer than two hundred sentences.[3] Hamilton's essay is impressionistic, and, although he is largely concerned with describing and criticizing examples of 'Milton's typical sentence',[4] he does nothing to demonstrate that the sentences he extracts for comment are genuinely representative. Stavely, too, adopts the impressionistic approach, developing what he presents as a thoroughgoing account of Milton's prose through lengthy explication of a score or so sentences from each period of his writing.

All write with confidence about what they consider quintessentially Miltonic in his sentence structure, and, like most critics who have considered this aspect of his prose even in passing, they find it particularly idiosyncratic. To Hamilton, his sentence structure shows that 'he is important as one of those writers who have striven . . . to bend the English language to their will'.[5] The others would endorse his verdict. However, comparison with a wider and more rational selection of writers than these critics use strongly suggests that many of his apparent peculiarities are common to others, and that, though there are minor differences, his preferences in sentence structure would not have seemed as unusual and remarkable to his contemporaries as they have generally done to his modern critics.

My study is based on the analysis of more than a thousand sentences, fifty from each of the pamphlets treated in earlier chapters. Sample size was once more determined by the length of the shortest tracts and by the common-sense assumption that a trait, if important, would be apparent within ten quarto pages or so of the text, which is generally the length of the samples in the Miltonic tracts. I took samples from the beginning of pamphlets. I found no great distinction between the two versions of *Readie and Easie Way*, and all findings and references are to the second edition.

It is a critical commonplace that Milton favoured 'the long, often inordinately long, sentence'.[6] Indeed, his stringent observations on Hall's 'curtall gibes, by one who makes his sentences by the Statute, as if all above three inches long were confiscat' (*Apology*, I, 873), and on the Modest Confuter who 'sobs me out halfe a dozen tizicall mottoes where ever he had them' and 'instead of well siz'd periods . . . greets us with a quantity of thum-ring posies' (ibid., p. 908) are almost as frequently quoted as his notorious dismissal of the work of his left hand. Emma, while conceding that the average length of Milton's prose sentences is shorter than Caxton's, notes also that Eliot averages eighteen words per sentence, Shakespeare eleven, Milton, in prose, fifty-three (p. 142). My own findings are set out in Table 8.[7]

I have attempted to determine the distribution of various sentence lengths. A number of points emerge. Hall's pamphlets and the *Modest Confutation* are plainly distinguished from most other tracts by the high incidence of sentences containing twenty or fewer words. Indeed, over a third of sentences in the sample from *Short Answer* have fewer than ten words. The validity of Milton's dislike of phthisical prose can be judged from passages like ' . . . *it is all one, so long as he is namelese; if he be a Consul, they are Senators; Civility is but a Ceremony; All faces under masks are alike; It matters not for the person . . .*' (*Short Answer*, sig. A3v). Here there are five syntactically independent units, five sentences. Although they are links in a chain of argument, Hall has severed the syntactical connections most writers would have made between them. The result is an unnatural prose. The reader's mind is synthesizing units which Hall has deliberatly separated, and the effect is an uncomfortable one of form quarrelling with content.

The only other pamphlets to show a penchant for sentences with twenty or fewer words are Milton's *Animadversions* and *Of True Religion*. That almost half the sentences in the former should be so short reflects, I believe, the format Milton selected for debate. It is, of course, a disputation between himself and Bishop Hall, in which a sentence or two from his opponent is followed by a generally brief observation or retort. These replies often take the form of questions or commands either to the reader or to Hall, and the high incidence of short sentences is largely because the interrogative and imperative moods do not

TABLE 8

Distribution of sentences according to sentence length (in words) in 50-sentence samples from first and final groups

	1-10 words	11-20	21-30	31-40	41-50	51-60	61-70	71-80	81-90	91-100	101-150	151-200	201-300	over 300
Miltonic: first group														
Of Reformation	6	3	9	4	4	5	2	3	2	3	7	1	1	-
Prelatical Episcopacy	3	6	11	9	2	2	3	1	-	3	7	3	-	-
Animadversions	11	12	8	5	4	2	-	-	1	1	3	1	2	-
Church-Government	2	4	5	7	5	8	3	2	2	1	8	2	1	-
Apology		3	8	6	6	8	6	2	1	1	7	2	-	-
Miltonic: final group														
Civil Power	1	6	10	8	4	2	3	2	2	2	8	2	-	-
Hirelings	1	7	8	7	4	5	6	1	-	2	5	3	1	-
Redie and Easie Way	1	3	4	7	4	5	8	4	2	2	6	1	1	2
Brief Notes	1	6	8	6	3	9	5	4	4	-	3	1	-	-
Of True Religion	3	14	9	9	6	2	3	1	2	-	1	-	-	-
Non-Miltonic: first group														
Humble Remonstrance	1	16	9	6	3	7	-	2	-	-	1	5	-	-
Defence of Humble Remonstrance	6	16	6	6	6	6	-	-	-	-	4	-	-	-
Short Answer	18	12	13	1	2	1	-	1	2	-	-	-	-	-
Answer to Humble Remonstrance	3	1	5	2	11	2	12	3	-	1	7	3	-	-
Vindication of Answer	6	9	7	7	5	4	6	2	1	-	2	1	-	-
Modest Confutation	14	9	7	4	5	4	2	-	1	3	-	1	-	-
Non-Miltonic: final group														
Dignity of Kingship	-	2	3	8	5	6	6	4	1	1	6	3	3	2
Brief Necessary Vindication	3	1	6	4	7	9	4	2	-	3	6	3	2	-
Interest	1	5	5	6	6	4	5	1	2	-	13	1	1	-
Good Old Cause	-	9	12	7	3	4	6	-	1	4	3	-	-	1

on the whole lend themselves to complex expression. Hence, for example:

Remonst. [i.e. Hall] But could they say my name is Legion; for wee are many.
Answ. Wherefore should you begin with the Devils name descanting upon the number of your opponents? wherefore that conceit of *Legion* with a by-wipe? (*Animadversions*, I, 665),

and

Remonst. I doe gladly fly to the barre.
Answ. To the barre with him then. Gladly you say (ibid., p. 666).

The atypical distribution of *Of True Religion*, however, can only be explained in terms of a major shift in Milton's practice. It is, of course, a much later tract than the others in the final group.

In general, the commonest sentence in Milton is that having between twenty-one and thirty words. Indeed, Milton does at both periods generate a fair number of long sentences. In most Miltonic samples between 18 per cent and 25 per cent of his sentences have more than one hundred words. But, though this clearly distinguishes his style from that of Hall and the Modest Confuter, it is a feature he has in common with Nedham, Prynne, 'G.S.', and the first Smectymnuan pamphlet. Against this background of contemporary practice the most notorious and blatant feature of his style appears decidedly less idiosyncratic. The evidence suggests that it is Hall and the Modest Confuter who are out of step with the norms of the genre. Perhaps it is worth observing that, though Milton has a number of points to make about their sentence structure, the Modest Confuter has nothing to say about his.

Sentence length, however, is but one, relatively dull aspect of sentence structure. Considerable critical discussion has focused on the extent to which Milton's prose is periodic. Progress has been hampered by general disagreement about what the term 'periodic' means. Wilkinson points out that there was a 'certain doubt' about what constituted a period in the classical era.[8] I suspect that Milton in the phrase 'well siz'd periods' (quoted above, p. 32) probably meant no more than 'fairly long sentences'. Recently the term has been used to mean a structure consisting of a number of sentences.[9] Emma and Hamilton use the term to mean sentences that have the main clause postponed or interrupted, though they perhaps apply the word slightly differently. The latter sees a distinction between the 'Ciceronian' period, in which 'the idea is introduced, then expanded and qualified through a complex of closely integrated dependent clauses, before being completed or resolved only as the sentence comes to an end', and the 'type of sentence that is periodic in the sense of delaying the completion of the central idea, without achieving the "circular" structure of the Ciceronian period'.[10] The distinction is very hard to apply in quantitative analysis. After all, the ideas of no sentence are completed until the sentence is completed—unless the sentence ends in nonsense! Furthermore, it requires for consideration of the syntactical feature of sentence structure the highly subjective interpretation of a different linguistic level in order to establish what may be the 'central idea'. Stavely largely follows Hamilton.[11] Emma evolves degrees of periodicity and attempts quantification under such impossibly indistinct categories as 'the mainly loose, partly periodic sentence' and 'the mainly periodic, partly loose sentence' (pp. 149-51).

However, it is clear what they are attempting, and the objective is a valid one. They are concerned with the position of subordinate clauses with respect to main clauses. The mist of critical imprecision can, I believe, be dispelled if we abandon the hand-me-down terminology of a rhetoric devised to describe and prescribe practice in an alien language, and adopt instead the transformational-generative model Ohmann has suggested in his discussion of Henry James's style.[12]

Transformational-generative grammar notes three principal ways in which subordinate material can relate to the main clause of a sentence. It can come before the main clause, as in 'After we went home, the other guests talked about us.' This is termed 'left-branching'. It can come after, as in 'The other guests talked about us, after we went home.' This is termed 'right-branching'. Finally, it can be placed within the main clause, as in 'The other guests, after we went home, talked about us'—'self-embedding'. What critics probably mean when they talk about 'periodic' prose is a style in which the main clauses of the sentences are postponed or interrupted by left-branching or self-embedding material without being followed by right-branching clauses. Seen in these clear and precise terms, this aspect of structure is genuinely tractable to quantification.

TABLE 9

Number of subordinate clauses directly dependent on main clauses in 50-sentence samples from first and final groups

	left-branching	right-branching	self-embedding
Miltonic: first group			
Of Reformation	19	73	5
Prelatical Episcopacy	15	61	9
Animadversions	10	52	3
Church-Government	23	62	16
Apology	33	62	7
Miltonic: final group			
Civil Power	20	54	7
Hirelings	20	52	20
Readie and Easie Way	19	81	16
Brief Notes	14	55	7
Of True Religion	12	64	2
Non-Miltonic: first group			
Humble Remonstrance	17	55	10
Defence of Humble Remonstrance	11	44	5
Short Answer	10	33	5
Answer to Humble Remonstrance	17	56	8
Vindication of Answer	14	54	5
Modest Confutation	10	54	12
Non-Miltonic: final group			
Dignity of Kingship	28	86	11
Brief Necessary Vindication	7	82	22
Interest	22	66	7
Good Old Cause	14	53	15

Table 9 presents information about how, within the fifty-sentence samples, subordinate clauses relate to main clauses. (Clauses which are in turn dependent on subordinate clauses are here discounted.) Milton shows no consistent preference for left-branching or self-embedding subordination at either period of his career. Certainly, the proportion of such constructions among his subordinated clauses does not differ radically from that of his contemporaries.

TABLE 10
Number of sentences terminating with main clauses in 50-sentence samples from first and final groups

Miltonic: first group
Of Reformation	1
Prelatical Episcopacy	2
Animadversions	1
Church-Government	6
Apology	4

Miltonic: final group
Civil Power	4
Hirelings	6
Readie and Easie Way	6
Brief Notes	7
Of True Religion	6

Non-Miltonic: first group
Humble Remonstrance	5
Defence of Humble Remonstrance	4
Short Answer	11
Answer to Humble Remonstrance	4
Vindication of Answer	5
Modest Confutation	4

Non-Miltonic: final group
Dignity of Kingship	4
Brief Necessary Vindication	6
Interest	9
Good Old Cause	5

Table 10 shows how many sentences within the samples terminate with a postponed or interrupted main clause. Simple sentences, of course, are excluded. Once more the evidence strongly suggests that this feature does not distinguish Milton's prose from that of his contemporaries. If by a periodic writer we mean one who favours left-branching or self-embedding subordination and who favours terminating sentences with postponed or interrupted main clauses, the term cannot be applied to Milton.

However, traditional critical concern with the elaborate structure of Milton's sentences is not completely misplaced. Milton's prose in both periods manifests a clausal complexity which to a limited degree sets it apart from most of the contemporaries I have considered. This complexity is not directly reflected in sentence length, perhaps because of Milton's enthusiasm for participial constructions (above, p. 27). Nor, as we have seen, does it lie in the disposition of subordinate material with respect to main clauses. It is rather the product of two features, the tendency to make a number of subordinate clauses depend on the same main clause, and the tendency to generate subordinate clauses which themselves support a number of further subordinate clauses. However, it is imperative that we do not overstate how sharply these features distinguish him from most of his contemporaries.

TABLE 11

Number of main clauses in 50-sentence samples from first and final groups having 3, 4 or 5 + subordinate clauses directly dependent on them

	3 clauses	4 clauses	5 + clauses	Total
Miltonic: first group				
Of Reformation	5	3	1	9
Prelatical Episcopacy	5	1	1	7
Animadversions	1	1	2	4
Church-Government	9	1	1	11
Apology	10	3	2	15
Miltonic: final group				
Civil Power	8	1	2	11
Hirelings	6	1	2	9
Readie and Easie Way	8	2	3	13
Brief Notes	4	0	0	4
Of True Religion	5	1	1	7
Non-Miltonic: first group				
Humble Remonstrance	3	0	2	5
Defence of Humble Remonstrance	2	1	0	3
Short Answer	0	0	0	0
Answer to Humble Remonstrance	5	1	0	6
Vindication of Answer	2	0	0	2
Modest Confutation	2	3	0	5
Non-Miltronic: final group				
Dignity of Kingship	11	5	0	16
Brief Necessary Vindication	7	3	3	13
Interest	3	4	1	8
Good Old Cause	5	0	0	5

In Table 11 I have recorded how many main clauses within the samples support three or more clauses that are immediately dependent upon them. Sentences that contain this sort of multi-branching around the main clause seem rather more a feature of Milton than of most contemporaries. *Animadversions*, which has an atypical proportion of short sentences, falls outside his general range. More puzzlingly, so too does *Brief Notes*. Also, it must be remembered that this feature is found in most of the others to some extent and is as prominent in 'G.S.', Nedham, and Prynne as in Milton.

Multi-branching suggests an effort to see actions in terms of their causality and implications and to follow ideas through their ultimate ramifications. The following is a relatively straightforward example of this kind of complex structure:

Whereas a modest title should only informe the buyer what the book containes without furder insinuation, this officious epithet so hastily assuming the modesty wch others are to judge of by reading, not the author to anticipate to himselfe by forestalling, is a strong presumption that this modesty set there to sale in the frontispice, is not much addicted to blush (*Apology*, I, 876).

The left-branching clause, 'whereas a modest . . . furder insinuation', itself supporting qualification, establishes the norm from which the Modest Confuter errs and sets up the criticism that Milton is to make. The self-embedding 'so hastily . . . forestalling', again itself subject to development and qualification, states the features that distinguish the title under attack. Finally, the right-branching element, 'that this modesty . . . blush', states the conclusions Milton would have us draw. It contrasts interestingly with the passage from Hall's *Short Answer* quoted earlier in this chapter (p. 32). Whereas Hall breaks up logically related elements, Milton tries to synthesize them into a complex whole.

The second characteristic of Milton's sentence structure is his tendency to generate further dependent clauses within clauses which are themselves subordinate. Table 12 shows how many clauses contain three or more such dependent elements within them. Again, it must be noted that this trait appears strongly in the first Smectymnuan tract, *Dignity of Kingship* and *Interest*. Prynne and Stubbe come close. *Animadversions* shows some aberration, for reasons already considered, as does *Of True Religion*. The high incidence of the feature in most Miltonic pamphlets, however, probably remains to a limited extent noteworthy.

TABLE 12

Number of subordinate clauses in 50-sentence samples from first and final groups directly dependent on main clauses and supporting 3, 4 or 5 + subordinate clauses

	3 clauses	4 clauses	5 + clauses	Total
Miltonic: first group				
Of Reformation	7	7	20	34
Prelatical Episcopacy	6	7	15	28
Animadversions	4	2	10	16
Church-Government	9	5	9	23
Apology	16	6	12	34
Miltonic: final group				
Civil Power	10	3	20	33
Hirelings	8	4	10	22
Readie and Easie Way	12	3	19	34
Brief Notes	6	7	12	25
True Religion	4	4	5	13
Non-Miltonic: first group				
Humble Remonstrance	9	3	5	17
Defence of Humble Remonstrance	6	2	7	15
Short Answer	3	3	5	11
Answer to Humble Remonstrance	10	4	18	32
Vindication of Answer	6	1	7	14
Modest Confutation	5	0	1	6
Non-Miltonic: final group				
Dignity of Kingship	9	6	17	32
Brief Necessary Vindication	7	4	8	19
Interest	7	4	15	26
Good Old Cause	8	4	8	20

Sometimes the principal subordinate clauses have a number of directly appended subordinates, as in:

. . . *of Christian liberty I write now; which others long since having don with all freedom under heathen emperors, I should do wrong to suspect, that I now shall with less under Christian governors, and such especially as profess openly thir defence of Christian libertie; although I write this not otherwise appointed or induc'd then by an inward perswasion* . . . (*Civil Power*, VII, 243-4).

Here the clause 'I should do wrong to suspect' supports a structure not unlike that of the main clause from *Apology* analysed above. The left-branching 'others . . . emperors' establishes the frame for comparison, the right-branching 'that I . . . of Christian libertie' states the fear discounted, and the futher right-branching 'although I write . . .' introduces a reservation which his avowed optimism leads him to disregard. More often, however, these supercharged subordinate clauses have a different structure. Clause supports clause, which supports clause, and so on, sometimes through a syntactical chain that is more than half a dozen units long, as in:

Now come the Epistles of *Ignatius* to shew us first, that *Onesimus* was Bishop of *Ephesus*; next to assert the difference of *Bishop* and *Presbyter*, wherin I wonder that men teachers of the Protestant Religion, make no difficulty of imposing upon our belief a supposititious ofspring of some dozen Epistles, whereof five are rejected as spurious, containing in them Heresies and trifles, which cannot agree in Chronologie with *Ignatius*, entitling him Arch-Bishop of *Antioch Theopolis*, which name of *Theopolis* that City had not till *Iustinians* time long after, as *Cedrenus* mentions, which argues both the barbarous time, and the unskilfull fraud of him that foisted this Epistle upon *Ignatius* (*Prelatical Episcopacy*, I, 635-6).

Clause right-branches from clause as Milton inexorably induces information, demonstrating the untrustworthiness of Ignatius' epistles. There is a persistent, relentless quality about this structure. Like the jaws of a bulldog, Milton closes tighter and tighter on his argument.

Of True Religion, of course a decidedly later pamphlet than the rest of the final group, shows certain distinct differences from the other Miltonic tracts. Milton evidently evolved an altogether simpler style. Although the practice of appending a number of clauses to a main clause persists, he no longer likes to pursue his point through heavy chains of linked clauses and, of course, sentence length declines sharply.

Clearly, sentence structure is not an aspect of style that distinguishes the early from the late Milton (except for his final tract), nor does it separate him from contemporary writers as sharply as other features do. He obviously differs from Hall and the Modest Confuter, but it is more difficult to distinguish him from the rest. As with the syntactical features considered in the previous chapter, the scope for idiosyncrasy and innovation in the mid-seventeenth century was perhaps slighter than in lexis or, to anticipate, in imagery. Although previous studies have made much of Milton's supposed abnormalities, the evidence I have assembled strongly suggests that, though he favoured a couple of constructions perhaps more than most, there is nothing about the syntax of a characteristic Miltonic sentence which would have seemed unusual, exceptional, or outrageous to his original readers.

5. IMAGERY

My study of Milton's imagery owes most to Clemen and Brooke-Rose. The former draws attention to the ways in which differently structured imagery determines differences in the textures of Shakespeare's plays.[1] The latter evolves an exhaustive systematization of the ways in which vehicle can link with tenor.[2] My concerns here are similarly not with the content of imagery, but with its frequency and form, with the way in which the texture of texts is determined by the density and structure of the imagery.

The notion of density implies an element of quantification and it is easier to talk about the relative incidence of various image-structures within a quantitative framework. However, we must be clear about the status of the quantification in the chapters on imagery. Exhaustive data cannot be objectively collected as for word frequency or most aspects of syntax. I adopt a very restricted definition of 'imagery'. I use it as a generic term for simile, metaphor, and other structures of comparison, such as those introduced by 'as if' or by 'as . . . (high/happy/small/etc.) . . . as'. Nevertheless, a high degree of subjectivity enters in deciding whether a feature can be regarded as an image at all.

As the classical rhetoricians appreciated, metaphor is a major way in which language expands.[3] Therefore, it is important to decide, when analysing imagery, whether the word re-applied is used metaphorically or whether it is used because it has become a normal term for the thing alluded to. The dynamics of language are such that the process whereby the metaphors become frozen is sometimes rapid—among other things, it depends on how often the new application is made—and the status of a word may well vary from generation to generation and even between contemporaries. For example, Hawkes is prepared to regard 'bonnet' in 'It's what's under the bonnet that counts!' (a quotation from a car advertisement) as metaphorical,[4] whereas on reading that I no more think of women's hats than I think of monks when I read of 'engine cowls'. It is very difficult indeed to estimate the way in which Milton's contemporaries regarded quite a lot of words that had extended their meanings by meta-

phorical application. All one can rely on is the limited evidence
of the *OED* and one's personal judgement.

Perhaps more surprisingly, there is a similar difficulty in
deciding what is or is not a simile. Analogies and precedents can
have the same basic structures as similes. For example, if I say,
'Cecil Rhodes was like Romulus', that may usefully be regarded
as a simile, but if I say, 'Remus was like Romulus', that could
not usefully be regarded as imagery. Again, one must rely on
one's judgement, and another may disagree with the decisions I
make.

So why then bother with quantification when the precision
and objectivity, which elsewhere are among its principal advantages, cannot be realized? There remain two principal advantages. Quantification shows, if perhaps approximately, the
extent to which phenomena occur—something which is not
always easy to gather from many stylistic studies. Secondly, my
decisions, if they diverge from my reader's, will, I hope, diverge
in roughly the same way in all the pamphlets considered, so that
it will be possible to show the importance, relative to each other,
of each feature in the various tracts.

Table 13 shows the density of imagery in the Miltonic and
non-Miltonic tracts of the first and last periods. Density is
expressed in terms of the numbers of images (vehicles) per thousand words of text. Quoted material not woven into the fabric of
the discourse is, of course, discounted in the calculation of
pamphlet length.

Here we may discern a clear and dramatic shift in Milton's
practice. His anti-prelatical tracts have a higher—sometimes
very much higher—incidence of imagery than other contributions to the Smectymnuan controversy. In his last tracts, this
falls away sharply. The fall seems to reflect no distinct trend in
the norms of the genre. Nevertheless, *Readie and Easie Way*
appears once more to be atypical of Milton's final tracts. The
first edition contains rather more imagery than other late
Miltonic pamphlets, and the distinction is sharpened in the
second edition, in which Milton introduces new material supercharged with imagery. Just as its higher word frequency harks
back to the practice of the anti-prelatical tracts, so, too, Milton
returns, perhaps in a conscious attempt to recapture the language of the *Good Old Cause*, to the image density of his early

TABLE 13

Incidence of imagery (including biblical imagery)
in first and final groups (expressed as number of images
(vehicles) per thousand words of text)

Miltonic: first group
   Of Reformation   7.5
   Prelatical Episcopacy   5.8
   Animadversions   8.8
   Church-Government   5.6
   Apology   5.3

Miltonic: final group
   Civil Power   3.0
   Hirelings   2.6
   Readie and Easie Way (1st edn.)   4.0
   Readie and Easie Way (2nd edn.)   5.1
   Brief Notes   2.6
   Of True Religion   2.7

Non-Miltonic: first group
   Humble Remonstrance   4.9
   Defence of Humble Remonstrance   2.2
   Short Answer   2.0
   Answer to Humble Remonstrance   1.9
   Vindication of Answer   1.7
   Modest Confutation   5.0

Non-Miltonic: final group
   Dignity of Kingship   4.1
   Brief Necessary Vindication   2.4
   Interest   3.1
   Good Old Cause   1.5

writing, and in the crisis breaking around the second edition, he screws this old-style figurative writing a pitch higher. In general, however, the style of his last tracts is marked by a decided shift from figurative writing towards literalness and plainness.

Imagery which draws upon the Bible, either through reference to scriptural matters in the vehicles or else through the adoption of biblical vehicles, poses interesting structural possibilities and variants, and is considered separately below.

I have attempted to categorize the remaining imagery in a system loosely based on that of Brooke-Rose. One fascinating shift in Miltonic practice emerges. Table 14 shows the relative incidence of what I term 'simple-substitution' and 'extended-

TABLE 14

*Extended-substitution imagery expressed as a
proportion of simple-substitution imagery in the first
and final groups (extended substitutions ÷ simple substitutions)*

Miltonic: first group	
Of Reformation	3.2
Prelatical Episcopacy	1.8
Animadversions	2.9
Church-Government	2.9
Apology	2.5
Miltonic: final group	
Civil Power	0.6
Hirelings	0.3
Readie and Easie Way (1st edn.)	1.5
Readie and Easie Way (2nd edn.)	1.0
Brief Notes	2.0
Of True Religion	1.0
Non-Miltonic: first group	
Humble Remonstrance	5.0
Defence of Humble Remonstrance	1.6
Short Answer	2.8
Answer to Humble Remonstrance	0.4
Vindication of Answer	2.1
Modest Confutation	2.8
Non-Miltonic: final group	
Dignity of Kingship	1.8
Brief Necessary Vindication	1.3
Interest	1.7
Good Old Cause	0.8

substitution imagery' in Milton and his contemporaries. By
'simple-substitution imagery' I mean imagery in which one
metaphorical term replaces a term of the tenor, but the substitution extends no further. Either the subject, verb, object, or
some other grammatical unit, unlike other units within the
structure, is non-literal. Thus, for example, in 'But let us not for
feare of a scarre-crow, or else through hatred to be reform'd
stand hankering and politizing' (*Of Reformation*, I, 610), 'scarre-
crow' is a metaphor for some previously stated and unfounded
fear, but the metaphor does not extend to other elements in the
grammatical structure. By 'extended-substitution imagery' I
mean imagery in which the metaphor extends beyond one

element, as in 'others belching the soure Crudities of yesterdayes *Poperie*' (ibid., p. 540), where both the vestiges of popery ('Crudities') and the means of reproducing them ('belching') are expressed in the vehicle.

It is clear from Table 14 that Milton shows a declining enthusiasm for the more complex of the metaphoric structures at the later period. This trend follows no clear pattern among the contemporaries. *Brief Notes* appears aberrant, but we are here discussing but a handful of examples. Clearly, in the early period Milton is willing to allow the vehicle to expand and cover more elements in one tenor. This shift is an important determinant of the general effect of the style of each period.

Simple-substitution imagery has an immediate lucidity and accuracy, a plainness and, though not necessarily dull, it gives the impression of being part of a medium suited to the precise transmission of fact and argument. Sometimes Milton's simple metaphor has the advantages of brevity as well as making an abstract concept concrete. Thus, in the phrase 'how uneffectual and weak is outward force with all her boistrous[5] tooles' (*Civil Power*, VII, 259), 'boistrous tooles' is much pithier as well as more concrete than any accurate alternative. Also, it compels a slight semantic adjustment—we are invited to regard 'force', the user of the tools, as partially personified in that normally only humans use tools. Milton, however, does not labour the point.

Some of his simple-substitution images have a considerable neatness and polish. Milton ridicules free parliaments that 'sit a whole year lieger in one place, only now and then to hold up a forrest of fingers' (*Readie and Easie Way*, second edition only, VII, 441). Here the very remoteness of the vehicle, 'forrest', from the verb and other elements is responsible for its comic incongruity. It is a subtle touch. Perhaps more typical of the character of simple substitution is 'a late parlament recovered the civil liberty of marriage from thir incroachment; and transferrd the ratifying and registring thereof from the canonical shop to the proper cognisance of civil magistrates' (*Hirelings*, VII, 300). The simple image of the shop scores its point efficiently—a neat identification of the clergy and shopkeepers—but the image does not disrupt the flow of apparently factual exposition or introduce material of which the conceptual relevance may not be immediately obvious. Milton still seems to be expounding hard facts.

Extended substitution creates a different impression. The precise conceptual relevance of each additional metaphoric element, though not necessarily less, may well be less immediately apprehended. The vehicle may assume an interest of its own, in part independent of the tenor. The reader's consideration of fact or argument slackens as he ponders the relevance or appreciates the beauty or ingenuity of the image. Consider, for example:

. . . finding the ease she [the soul] had from her visible, and sensuous collegue the body in performance of *Religious* duties, her pineons now broken, and flagging, [she] shifted off from her selfe, the labour of high soaring any more, forgot her heavenly flight, and left the dull, and droyling carcas to plod on in the old rode, and drudging Trade of outward conformity (*Of Reformation*, I, 522).

Despite the appositional 'the body' and such linking mechanisms as 'heavenly' and 'of outward conformity', it remains puzzling how some of the details relate to the tenor. What are the 'pineons'? Are we to accept them simply as a feature of the vehicle narrative? Or perhaps we are to identify them with that which helps the soul to heaven, faith maybe, or good works. Certainly, the image of the struggling, overweight bird rivets the imagination, but it is, perhaps, at the expense of clarity and efficiency. Mental focus on Milton's argument is relaxed. The reader forgets about the soul in concentration on the fate of the bird. The chain of factual or quasi-factual exposition has been broken.

This image points up sharply the difference between a style that favours simple substitutions and one that favours greater metaphoric elaboration. Of course, there are some extended substitutions in the later tracts, and these, too, invite the reader temporarily to switch focus from tenor to vehicle, though, as I shall argue, none have the immense imaginative appeal as this from *Of Reformation*. None the less, it is true to say that quantification establishes a distinct shift.

Quantification, however, can provide no springboard into discussion of many of the most interesting aspects of imagery, such as its scope, nor can it indicate its brilliance.

The imagery of Milton's anti-prelatical tracts frequently assumes a strong dramatic or narrative quality. A complete action is described within the vehicle. He relates a continuous narrative or else creates a short drama, a cameo, with an interest and a continuity that are to an extent independent of the tenor. For example, he compares his refutation of the historical arguments for prelacy based on the example of Leontius, Bishop of Magnesia, to the dismissal of this supposed precedent's ghost: 'we shall doe better not to detain this venerable apparition of *Leontius* any longer, but dismiss him with his List of seven and twenty [bishops following Titus], to sleep unmolested in his former obscurity'[6] (*Prelatical Episcopacy*, I, 631-2). Milton creates a little scene in which Leontius, for all his dignity, is sent back, clutching his spurned list, to the dark corner where he slept. Again, Hall had made much of the idea of the Mother Church, of which he was the loyal son[7] and the Smectymnuans the undutiful children.[8] Milton fleshes out the imaginary ménage, casting the prelates as this mother's paramours. He sketches the scenario for a domestic drama:

And if we come to ask a reason of ought from our deare mother, she's invisible, under the lock and key of the Prelates her spirituall adulterers, the onely are the internuntio's or the go-betweens of this trim devis'd mummery: whatsoever they say she sayes, must be a deadly sin of disobedience not to beleeve (*Animadversions*, I, 728).

Note, especially, the word 'mummery'.[9] Milton explicitly acknowledges the affinities between a dramatic presentation and the scene he is describing as a metaphoric statement of the role of the prelacy in the Church.

Examples of imagery in which the vehicle narrates a complete action or depicts something like a dramatic scene occur frequently in the anti-prelatical tracts—Truth needing to prove herself a retainer of Constantine or produce a chit of recommendation from Cranmer (*Of Reformation*, I, 535); the fable of Io, told to describe the abuse done to the commonwealth (ibid., p. 572); the physicians of London depicted as attempting to cure diseases by lecturing on them from the pulpit, intended to parallel the uselessness of preaching without discipline (*Church-Government*, I, 756); the leisurely anecdote about the parvenu gardener (the prelate) and the 'honest and laborious' gardener (the true Christian minister) (*Animadversions*, I, 716-7); the Modest Confuter judging his adversaries before the jury of readers has been impanelled (*Apology*, I, 876). This list, of course, is illustrative rather than exhaustive.

This quality is not found in the longer imagery of Milton's later tracts. When images are expanded, they generally assume a schematism that dispels their narrative or dramatic impact, as in, 'The ship of the Commonwealth is alwaies under sail; they sit at the stern; and if they stear well, what need is ther to change them; it being rather dangerous?' (*Readie and Easie Way*, VII, 433-4; also first edition, p. 369). This passage can usefully be compared with an earlier image in which he also likens the state to a ship (it is, of course, a very common motif in the political literature of the sixteenth and seventeenth centuries):

To be plainer Sir, how to soder, how to stop a leak, how to keep up the floting carcas of a crazie, and diseased Monarchy, or State betwixt wind, and water, swimming still upon her own dead lees, that now is the deepe designe of a politician (*Of Reformation*, I, 572).

Knights, in his well-known essay on Bacon, claims that, unlike the imagery of Hooker, Nashe, and Deloney, his shows no sensitive awareness of both sides of the image, of vehicle and tenor.[10] Some such distinction can be made between the imagery of the early and late Milton. In the example from *Readie and Easie Way*, the image functions conceptually but not imaginatively. It tersely expresses the relationship between state and governors, but tells us little about the ship, its crew, and its fate. Indeed, in the interest of clarifying the tenor it falsifies the nature of the vehicle. After all, no ship is always under sail, and every helmsman must be relieved some time! In contrast, the ship in *Of Reformation* is vividly realized. In the later prose imagery is more functional—a clear exposition that in no way detracts attention from what Milton would have us regard as hard fact. But it is much less imaginative.

Does the shift in Milton mirror some trend among the non-Miltonic pamphlets? Some imagery with a narrative or dramatic interest occurs in most of them. Hall relates 'the story that Plutarch tels of the contestation between *Crassus* and *Deiotarus*', complete with dialogue, as an image for his own battle in old age against the Smectymnuans (*Short Answer*, pp. 101-2). There are one or two such images in the tracts of the Smectymnuans them-

selves, such as a leisurely narrated anecdote about 'a painter
that limmed two pictures to the same proportion and figure' and
then altered one, which they use to describe the degeneration
of the bishops from their original form (*Answer to Humble
Remonstrance*, p. 77). The feature can be found, too, in the
pamphlets of the later group. For example, Nedham describes
the rescue of liberty, a 'tender Virgin', from the hands of her
ravishers (*Interest*, p. 22). Stubbe tells the story of how Cerberus
barked at the daylight when Theseus dragged him to the surface
as an analogy to the responses of the haters of liberty to the 'first
blushes of a *Commonwealth*' (*Good Old Cause*, sig. **3v). Again,
'G.S.' narrates the familiar fable of the frogs to illustrate the
shortcomings of the republican government on the Dutch model
(*Dignity of Kingship*, p. 114). However, it is clear that imagery
which establishes a dramatic scene or relates a complete action of
some narrative interest is decidedly less common in the Non-
Miltonic pamphlets than in Milton's anti-prelatical tracts. But it
is equally clear that such imagery does not disappear from the
writings of contemporaries in 1659 to 1660. Again , Milton's
development seems idiosyncratic.

In general, Milton's early imagery is more vivid and more
fully realized than his later, but very often the relation of vehicle
and tenor may be puzzling to determine, as in the bird-soul
image from *Of Reformation* considered above. Sometimes it is
clearly inappropriate to look for precise relevance for all the
details of vehicles in the early pamphlets. Describing prelatical
responses to revelations of their malpractices, Milton writes, 'O
what a death it is to the Prelates to be thus unvisarded, thus
uncas'd, to have the Periwigs pluk't off that cover your bald-
nesse, your inside nakednesse thrown open to publick view'
(*Animadversions*, I, 668). The three processes—unmasking, strip-
ping, removal of the wig—do not correlate with three separate
actions of exposing the prelates, but seem, rather, the elements
of a sadistic fantasy of humiliating reprisal. The detail and division give a stunning vigour to the vehicle, but they do not relate
conceptually to the tenor.

In contrast the imagery of Milton's later pamphlets has a
near-clinical precision. He no longer introduces detail into the
vehicles which cannot be tagged firmly to some element in the
tenor. Vehicles are rarely qualified beyond the meagrest of

adjectives and adverbs. We find occasional exceptions—'To persue them further through the obscure and intangld wood of antiquitie' (*Hirelings*, VII, 328) is perhaps reminiscent of the earlier Milton—but these are very infrequent. When he talks of 'a strange degenerate contagion' (*Readie and Easie Way*, VII, 422: the phrase is 'degenerate corruption' in the first edition, p. 357), the adjectives do not make the vehicle more vivid to the imagination. 'Degenerate contagion' clearly means 'contagion of degeneration'. The adjective must be pointing to the tenor—after all, strictly, a degenerate contagion would be a weakened and failing strain of a disease. Even 'guilded', in 'Yet neither shall we obtain or buy at an easie rate this new guilded yoke [monarchy restored] which thus transports us' (ibid., second edition only, p. 450), functions conceptually rather than sensuously, establishing the costliness of the yoke (and yokes, literally, are not costly) rather than the concrete details of its appearance.

The wealth of detail and description, which often makes the vehicles of Milton's early imagery so vivid and interesting, serves to distinguish it from the non-Miltonic imagery in general, as well as from his own practice in the last tracts. There are exceptions. Prynne tells us more about Otho's abdication (*Brief Necessary Vindication*, pp. 56-7) and 'G.S.' more about Ovid's exile (*Dignity of Kingship*, p. 115) than strictly necessary for them to make their point about the tenor. In general, however, among the non-Miltonic writers considered detail and description function only in relating vehicle to tenor. Over and over again the reader encounters imagery structurally similar to that of the later Miltonic tracts—imagery like 'the Iron and Insupportable yoake of this *Episcopall Government*' (*Answer to Humble Remonstrance*, pp. 14-15), 'our *bondage* under the *Norman* Yoak' (*Good Old Cause*, sig. *7v), 'the insupportable yoke of an absolute Monarchy' (*Interest*, p. 21), etc.

The imagery of the anti-prelatical pamphlets often enables Milton to make a series of related points within the framework of one vehicle. Thus, the image applied to Hall and his party: 'You will find some such as will prognosticate your date, and tell you that after your long *Summer Solstice* the *Aequator* calls for you, to reduce you to the ancient, and equall house of *Libra*' (*Animadversions*, I, 698), contains really two points—that the prelates have had a long period of prosperity which must inevitably decline (from the solstitial point there is no way they can rise, they can only fall away), and that they are now being brought to justice, for, as the Yale editor notes, 'the word "libra", a pair of scales, and the word "equal" both suggest the idea of justice' (ibid., n. 3). The extended fables of the wen and of the stone giant each make a series of related points. The former effectively suggests that prelacy is an ugly excrescence, that it wishes to establish itself as the head of the body politic and thinks too highly of its role, that it contributes nothing to the Common-wealth, and that it should be cut off and cut open (*Of Reformation*, I, 583-4). Similarly, to respect the arguments drawn from antiquity in preference to the evidence of the Bible is like wor-shipping an 'unactive, and livelesse *Colossus*'; it can impress only 'children, and weaklings'; it is marred when taken to pieces (that is, analysed stage by stage); the users of arguments drawn from antiquity must work 'with sweat and toile' to apply them; they can be crushed by the very bulk of antiquity; and it is all over-thrown by resort to the 'weapon' of scripture (*Animadversions*, I, 699-701). Again, in:

No, no, vaine Prelates, this was but as the Scaffolding of a new edifice which for the time must board, and overlooke the highest battlements, but if the structure once finish't, any passenger should fall in love with them, and pray that they might still stand, as being a singular grace, and strengthning to the house, who would otherwise thinke, but that the man were presently to be laid hold on, and sent to his friends and kindred (ibid., pp. 714-15),

Milton effectively gives a potted, Puritan history of Church government—the original role of the bishops in apostolic times, then redundancy and ugliness and the insanity of retaining them—scaffolding is not a grace and it is not a strengthening and neither are the bishops. Though Milton's famous image of the cooling pot (*Of Reformation*, I, 536) is certainly as vivid, sensu-ous, and naturalistic as critics have claimed,[11] the details he introduces also expand the image conceptually and widen the range of points he is making—not only do promoted clergymen lose their zeal, which they 'sensibly exhale and reake out', but they also settle 'at the top' (a reference to the ecclesiastical hier-archy) into an indolence represented by 'skinny congealment'.

However, this exciting element of the earlier prose imagery is not a major feature of Milton's later pamphlets. Once again, comparison with the non-Miltonic tracts indicates that this change in Milton is part of no general trend in the genre. For, although certainly others do not use much of this sort of imagery, it is to be found in both periods. Hall can produce:

> . . . *they tell you of raylings, revilings, scornings, never the like since* Montagues *Appeal: and present you with a whole bundle of such strange flowers of Rhetorick, as truly, I wondered should ever grow in my Garden: wherin, they have done passing wisely, in not noting the Pages, as the severall beds, wherin such rare plants grew: for I have carefully re-examined the Book, and profess seriously, that some of them I cannot finde at all . . . (Short Answer,* sig. A4r),

and the Smectymnuans have:

> But wee should be glad to know in what *Palace* that *Prelate* lives, that hath drawne out his assumed sword of discipline against these *unsound teachers?* Or if he hath drawne, hath strucke, or if strucke, hath not strucke with the backe; while the poore *Non conformists* hath beene slaine with the edge? (*Vindication of Answer*, p. 207).

There are a few examples from the later period, such as the following from *The Dignity of Kingship*:

> Some joynt Rules of *Confederacie*, the united *Provinces* . . . have made among themselves but indeed they are but as so many severall flowers pickt and made up into a *Nosegay*, which have no tye one to another, but a string about all, thus they were first united for fear of a *string* or *halter* . . . (p. 104),

which makes two points, about the disparate nature of the United Provinces and their motives for confederation. But as all three quoted passages show, when Milton's contemporaries try this sort of imagery, it has a tediously explicit and mechanical quality, as though they cannot trust themselves to fire the reader's imagination with a spontaneous awareness of extended correlations between vehicle and tenor. The vehicle does not develop organically but needs the prompting of the author, and hence clumsy phrases like 'not noting the Pages, as the severall beds' or the strained explanation of the significance of the 'string about it all'. They show no sensitivity for the vehicle—the Smec-

tymnuans can hardly decide how the 'sword of discipline' was
used, if it was used at all. However, though such imagery is
decidedly inferior to and less frequent than that of Milton in the
anti-prelatical tracts, at least it does not disappear, as it does in
Milton, in the later period.

Milton manifests further distinct shifts in structural preferences in the imagery he draws from the Bible. Its study, however, poses one or two further problems for the process of quantification. By 'biblical imagery', I mean any of three basic structures: imagery in which the vehicle is adopted from a vehicle in
the Bible and applied to the same tenor as it refers to biblically;
imagery drawn from a biblical vehicle but applied to a tenor
different from that to which it refers biblically; and finally
imagery in which the vehicle is drawn from some person, thing,
event, or concept occurring biblically. It must be recognized that
in culling out biblical imagery a further subjective element
enters. Readers may differ as to what the biblical allusion may
be; indeed, they may disagree about whether an image contains
any biblical allusion at all. For example, in the following:

. . . if repentance sent from heaven meet this lost wanderer, and draw
him out of that steep journey wherein he was hasting towards destruction, to come and reconcile to the Church, if he bring with him his bill
of health, and that he is now cleare of infection and of no danger to the
other sheep . . . (*Church-Government*, I, 848),

the Yale editor would see 'an allusion to the Gadarene swine:
Matthew 8:30-2; Mark 5:11-16; Luke 8:32-4' (ibid., n. 125). I
feel this invalid. The Miltonic image speaks of sheep, not swine,
and here a single animal is being saved, not a herd consigned to
destruction. I would prefer to regard it as an allusion to the Good
Shepherd's salvation of the lost sheep (Matt. 18:12-13, Luke
15:4-6). Yet I base my decision on a subjective evaluation of the
evidence, and no doubt others would disagree with some of the
allusions I identify.

There are further difficulties, perhaps needing no exempli-
fication, in distinguishing between imagery and the citation of
biblical precedent, and between imagery and the use of biblical
proof-texts. Both problems are particularly acute in Milton's
last group of texts and in Stubbe's *Good Old Cause*.

Quantification is thus even more beset with methodological problems than in the case of non-biblical imagery. None the less, I believe it remains a useful tool for showing, albeit only approximately, the relative incidence of phenomena.

The incidence of biblical imagery varies in no distinct pattern from pamphlet to pamphlet. Most Miltonic tracts from both periods have about a third of their vehicles drawn from biblical material. The range is from *Readie and Easie Way* (second edition) (17 per cent of all vehicles) to *Civil Power* (56 per cent). On average among the non-Miltonic texts about a quarter of vehicles are drawn from the Bible. The proportion of biblical material in the

TABLE 15

Images in the first and final groups that
have biblical sources precisely stated (expressed as percentage
of all biblical imagery)

	%
Miltonic: first group	
Of Reformation	—
Prelatical Episcopacy	—
Animadversions	5
Church-Government	—
Apology	—
Miltonic: final group	
Civil Power	37
Hirelings	22
Readie and Easie Way (1st edn.)	—
Readie and Easie Way (2nd edn.)	—
Brief Notes	—
Of True Religion	33
Non-Miltonic: first group	
Humble Remonstrance	—
Defence of Humble Remonstrance	—
Short Answer	—
Answer to Humble Remonstrance	9
Vindication of Answer	12
Modest Confutation	—
Non-Miltonic: final group	
Dignity of Kingship	—
Brief Necessary Vindication	36
Interest	—
Good Old Cause	16

non-Miltonic texts varies from 7 per cent of all vehicles (*Interest*) to 46 per cent (*Good Old Cause*).

In the early period, as Table 15 shows, Milton clearly regards the citation of the source of his biblical imagery as unimportant. Only in two places does he indicate chapter and verse from which he is borrowing and to which he is alluding, marginal attributions in *Animadversions* (I, 727 nn. 10 and 11). Elsewhere attribution is vaguer—'as *Salomon* saith . . .' (*Church-Government*, I, 819), 'as Saint *Paul* saith . . .' (*Apology*, I, 949), 'as God pronounces by *Isaiah* . . .' (*Animadversions*, I, 718), etc. In all I find less than a dozen examples of attribution, even as imprecise as

TABLE 16

*Biblical images exhibiting accurate quotation
in first and final groups (expressed as percentage of all
biblical imagery)*

	%
Miltonic: first group	
Of Reformation	—
Prelatical Episcopacy	—
Animadversions	5
Church-Government	3
Apology	8
Miltonic: final group	
Civil Power	21
Hirelings	28
Readie and Easie Way (1st edn.)	40
Readie and Easie Way (2nd edn.)	37
Brief Notes	—
Of True Religion	33
Non-Miltonic: first group	
Humble Remonstrance	
Defence of Humble Remonstrance	40
Short Answer	—
Answer to Humble Remonstrance	—
Vindication of Answer	12
Modest Confutation	12
Non-Miltonic: final group	
Dignity of Kingship	11
Brief Necessary Vindication	27
Interest	—
Good Old Cause	24

this, in the anti-prelatical tracts. In contrast, quite a high proportion of biblical images in the first two of his final period have a
precisely cited reference. Of the three images in *Of True Religion*,
one gives chapter and verse of origin (Columbia, VI, 174) and
another has the vaguer 'in the Psalmes' (ibid., p. 179). Moreover, roughly half the biblical vehicles of *Readie and Easie Way*
(both editions) have a vague reference of some sort.

Comparison with the non-Miltonic pamphlets proves instruc-
tive here. In each period some sometimes cite sources (the Smectymnuans, Prynne, and Stubbe), and some never cite them
(Hall, the Modest Confuter, 'G.S.', and Nedham). No general
development is to be discerned. The change in Milton's practice
represents a shift in his way of regarding the source, the Bible
itself. It does not reflect a development in the genre. Such citation of sources gives to his prose an appearance of accuracy and
authority, and perhaps points to a new care and sense of respon-
sibility in handling sacred material.

Table 16 shows how often Milton and others quote directly
from the Authorized Version of the Bible[12] when forming an
image from sacred material. Accurate quotation appears much
less frequently in the early Miltonic tracts. Then he freely alters
or tailors the biblical allusions to suit his purpose. Even when the
image is attributed and he is following the text closely, he will
conflate and adjust the material. Thus in the following:

. . . the call of wisdom and vertu may be heard every where, as *Salomon*
saith, *She crieth without, she uttereth her voice in the streets, in the top of high
places, in the chief concours, and in the openings of the Gates* (*Church-
Government*, I, 819),

though the typography implies that Milton is quoting verbatim,
he is, in fact, silently conflating two quite separate sources:

Prov. 1:20, Wisdom crieth without; she uttereth her voice in the
streets;

and

Prov. 8:1, Doth not wisdom cry, and understanding put forth her
voice?
          2, She standeth in the top of high places, by the way in the
places of the paths.

3, She crieth at the gates, at the entry of the city, at the coming in at the doors.

However, Milton does not exercise this sort of editorial freedom in his final group of pamphlets. He often preserves the wording of the Bible, in the Authorized Version, sometimes even when this causes a stylistic clumsiness or pleonasm which he could have easily avoided. Consider:

Not long after, as the apostles foretold, hirelings like wolves came in by herds, *Acts* 20. 29 *For, I know this, that after my departing shall greevous wolves enter in among you, not sparing the flock* (*Hirelings*, VII, 280).

TABLE 17
'Improved' vehicles in first and final
groups (expressed as percentage of all biblical imagery)

	%
Miltonic: first group	
Of Reformation	60
Prelatical Episcopacy	69
Animadversions	40
Church-Government	34
Apology	35
Miltonic: final group	
Civil Power	5
Hirelings	11
Readie and Easie Way (1st edn.)	20
Readie and Easie Way (2nd edn.)	12
Brief Notes	—
Of True Religion	—
Non-Miltonic: first group	
Humble Remonstrance	11
Defence of Humble Remonstrance	—
Short Answer	20
Answer to Humble Remonstrance	—
Vindication of Answer	15
Modest Confutation	6
Non-Miltonic: final group	
Dignity of Kingship	21
Brief Necessary Vindication	—
Interest	40
Good Old Cause	12

It is hard to believe that the allusion would have escaped recognition had Milton terminated it after 'herds'. It seems that Milton in the later pamphlets wishes to make clear, explicit, and precise relationships which earlier would have been left tacit and vaguely allusive, and hence this process of tying the biblical images to their sources with tight ligatures of close quotation from the contemporaneously most popular translation. Reference here to contemporaries is perhaps less useful than elsewhere, in that there has been no investigation into the Bible translation they favoured.

Table 17 shows the proportion of biblical imagery in which the vehicle has been 'improved', that is, made more dramatic or vivid or detailed than its scriptural source. The table also well exemplifies the limitations of quantification in literary criticism. A clear enough trend emerges. Milton in the early period, improves upon a substantial proportion of his biblical vehicles. This falls away drastically in the final period. From the non-Miltonic groups it appears that this shift is idiosyncratic in Milton, and that Milton in his anti-prelatical tracts improves upon a higher proportion of imagery than all except Nedham. However, since I attribute the same numerical value to all examples of the same feature, irrespective of disparities in artistic achievement, quantification can in no way suggest the superiority of the brilliant innovations and improvements of Milton's early tracts both over those of his later period and of other writers.

In describing the narrative techniques of the story of Abraham and Isaac, Auerbach perceptively notes:

In this atmosphere it is unthinkable that an implement, a landscape through which the travelers passed, the serving-men, or the ass, should be described, that their origin or descent or material or appearance or usefulness should be set forth in terms of praise; they do not even permit an adjective: they are serving-men, ass, wood, and knife, and nothing else, without an epithet; they are to serve the end which God has commanded; what in other respects they were, are, or will be, remains in darkness.[13]

The gnomic reticence which he identifies as characteristic of this section of Genesis, I believe, pervades most of the Bible, though there are perhaps exceptions such as the Song of Songs. Yet

Milton in his anti-prelatical tracts transmutes this almost
epithetless terseness into the same sort of vivid, luxuriant
imagery that he generates from other sources. Thus:

Matt. 7:26, And every one that heareth these sayings of mine, and
doeth them not, shall be likened unto a foolish man, which built his
house upon the sand:
        27, And the rain descended, and the floods came, and the
winds blew, and beat upon that house, and it fell: and great was the fall
of it

is rounded out into:

. . . the earnest desire which the Prelates have to build their Hierarchy
upon the sandy bottome of the law, gives us to see abundantly the little
assurance which they finde to reare up their high roofs by the autority
of the Gospell (*Church-Government*, I, 775).

Christ's parable tells us nothing about the foolish man's house.
Its specifications, apparently, do not matter. Milton adds the
detail 'reare up their high roofs', which at once makes it more
concrete and carries an extra moral weight. It connotes the prelates' pride. The house they raise is a lofty roof, a palace. Again,
the selection of the rather poetic verb 'rear'[14] heightens the
actions of Christ's 'foolish man' to a folly of more epic
proportions.

        Milton takes a Pauline image:

I Cor. 12:24, For our comely parts have no need: but God hath tem-
pered the body together, having given more abundant honour to that
part which lacked:
        27, Now ye are in the body of Christ, and the members in
particular.

From this he fashions 'then did the Spirit of unity and meeknesse
inspire, and animate every joynt, and sinew of the mysticall
body' (*Of Reformation*, I, 547). He replaces the vague, unspecific
'members' with the precise 'joynt and sinew', and he makes the
image more pregnant, more suggestive. God no longer
'tempers' the body, but the spirit breathes into it, animating the
whole as God animated Adam.

Sometimes his innovations recast the original completely,
Thus:

Matt. 13:30, Let both grow together until the harvest: and in the time
of harvest I will say to the reapers, Gather together first the tares, and
bind them in bundles to burn them: but gather the wheat into my barn

is re-utilized in the image: '[Anselm] little dreamt then that the
weeding-hook of reformation would after two ages pluck up his
glorious poppy [i.e. prelacy] from insulting over the good corne'
(*Church-Government*, I, 777). 'Gather' is replaced by the more
vigorous 'pluck up'. 'Tare' gives way to 'poppy', a naturalistic
detail—the poppy is common in English cornfields[15]—but one
which carries a moral weight, in that its scarlet gaudiness sym-
bolizes the spurious splendour of the prelates. 'Insulting',
apparently not normally collocated with non-human nouns, adds
a lexical brilliance. Similarly, 'Rev. 3:16, So then because thou
art lukewarm, and neither cold nor hot, I will spue thee out of my
mouth' becomes 'but their *devotion* most commonly comes to that
queazy temper of lukewarmnesse, that gives a Vomit to GOD
himselfe' (*Of Reformation*, I, 537), with the striking phrase
'queazy temper of lukewarmnesse' and the colloquial-sounding
'gives a Vomit', that is, administers an emetic.[16] Milton firmly
roots the image in the world of seventeenth-century kitchen-
physic.

The alterations to biblical imagery that Milton makes in his
last tracts are fewer and relatively trivial and reflect his general
movement towards austerity of style. For example, he calls
Gehazi a 'sharking minister' (*Hirelings*, VII, 297) and the man
who would build a tower (Luke 14:29-30) 'a foolish builder'
(*Readie and Easie Way*, VII, 422-3; first edition, p. 357). Among
the non-Miltonic writers, innovations appear on the whole of a
similarly limited scope. Only 'G.S.' attempts improvements of
the type Milton makes in his earlier tracts, and his lack of success
contrasts well with Milton's achievements. For example, he tries
to make stately and dramatic the plain

I Kgs. 12:7, And they spake unto him, saying, If thou wilt be a servant
unto this people this day , and wilt serve them, and answer them, and
speak good words to them, then they will be thy servants for ever.

But he produces instead the pompous and emptily wordy:

But as the old men said to *Rehoboam*, If your *wisdome* . . . find as speedy way of answering the *Nations* earnest hopes, and almost *impatient expectation*, your name will be not only *famous*, but your *person admired*, (even almost to adoration) . . . (*Dignity of Kingship*, p. 213, sig. p3r).

For the neatness and precision of the original 'G.S.' has substituted the high-flown inanity which he normally reserves for his addresses *in propria persona* to his beloved King.

In density, in structure, and in quality Milton's biblical and non-biblical imagery marks off his first group of tracts as stylistically quite different from his final pamphlets and distinguishes them sharply from comparable examples of mid-century prose.

6. CONCLUSIONS TO SECTION 1

In the light of the first part of this study certain critical orthodoxies about Milton's prose style would seem to be untenable. There is little evidence to suggest that Milton draws on vulgar registers or uses words of Latin origin in atavistic senses not current in seventeenth-century English. His characteristic sentence structure, emphatically, is not modelled on the Ciceronian period, nor are his sentences exceptionally long if they are viewed in the context of contemporary practice in the same genre. Many of Emma's conclusions about Milton's syntactical preferences seem unconvincing if his investigation is repeated on a sounder basis with larger samples and more carefully selected authors for comparison.

The lexis of Milton's anti-prelatical pamphlets distinguishes them sharply both from his last group and from the non-Miltonic tracts considered. In the early period he forms unusual collocations and generates interesting neologisms both by borrowing from foreign languages and from the native resources of English. This lexical brilliance is not paralleled in his last tracts, nor is it a feature of the contemporaries selected for comparison. A study of word frequencies reveals that in his anti-prelatical group Milton prefers to use a variety of synonyms for recurrent concepts whereas later the same words and phrases are likely to be reiterated. This shift in his practice does not seem to reflect a general change in the norms of the genre.

There are few elements in Milton's syntax that distinguish him from the mainstream of contemporary pamphleteers. In both periods he does show a predilection for participial constructions and his sentences in general show a high incidence of multibranching and heavy dependent clauses. In his last group he has a tendency to place adjectives behind the nouns to which they refer and to use fewer of them.

The density of imagery is decidedly higher in Milton's first group than in his last. Again, this reflects no distinct development in the genre. His anti-prelatical tracts in general have a higher incidence of imagery than the non-Miltonic pamphlets considered. Between the periods Milton's practice in adapting imagery from biblical sources alters in a number of interesting ways, perhaps pointing to some change in his attitude to sacred material. Again, the change is not paralleled in the other examples of the genre. The imagery, biblical and non-biblical, of Milton's first group has a brilliance not found elsewhere in the pamphlets considered in this section.

Milton's first group constitutes a stylistically homogeneous unit. Among his final tracts *Of True Religion*, which postdates the others by more than a decade, manifests a change towards a simpler sentence structure uncharacteristic of the other Miltonic tracts considered here. *Readie and Easie Way*, too is exceptional among the final group in that its image density, frequency of adjectives, and word frequency are more akin to the anti-prelatical tracts. This I interpret as Milton's attempt to revive the language and spirit of the Good Old Cause. In other features, however, it accords with his tracts of the period immediately before the Restoration.

Generally, then, a clear pattern of development can be discerned. The flamboyance and linguistic innovation of his anti-prelatical pamphlets is replaced by a more sober style, a plainer medium for exposition. Investigation into when and how these changes in the fabric of his prose occurred is the business of the second part of this study.

Section II: The Tracts of 1643 to 1645 and 1649

7. WORD FREQUENCIES

Table 18 presents the results of investigation into word frequencies in 3,000-word samples from the pamphlets of Milton's intermediate periods and from the contemporary tracts

TABLE 18
Word frequencies in samples from intervenient groups

	lexical words occurring once	total vocabulary
Miltonic: 1643-5		
Doctrine (1st edn.)	746	1,046
Doctrine (2nd edn.)	837	1,124
Of Education	828	1,117
Areopagitica	802	1,074
Tetrachordon	763	1,054
Colasterion	715	1,009
Miltonic: 1649		
Tenure	742	1,039
Observations	754	1,043
Eikonoklastes	737	1,024
Non-Miltonic: 1643-5		
Answer to a Book	443	758
Bloudy Tenent	654	991
Dippers Dipt	814	1,106
Mans Mortallitie	515	837
Non-Miltonic: 1649		
Eikon Alethine	727	1,026
Eikon Basilike	562	886
Golden Rule	618	941
Humble Address	532	834

selected for comparison. All the Miltonic works fall within the range of his anti-prelatical tracts and are again characterized by the use of more lexical items than most of the contemporary tracts analysed.[1]

As in his earlier tracts the word frequencies of both groups of Miltonic works seem shaped by his use of clusters of synonyms for recurrent concepts. Thus, from the tracts of 1643 to 1645, pupils in *Of Education* are variously termed 'children' (II, 372. 2), 'striplings' (p. 373. 1), 'novices' (p. 374. 10), and 'youth' (p. 376. 17). The author of *Answer to a Book* is termed 'Sollici-ter' (*Colasterion*, II, 727. 2), 'man of Law' (ibid.), '*Atturney*' (p. 729.6), 'hucster at Law' (ibid.), and '*Sub advocate*' (p. 730). Milton's enthusiasm for finding synonyms may well blind him to a distinction between 'attorney', that is, a man skilled in the practice of Common Law, and 'solicitor', one trained in the Law of Equity,[2] though in practice the same man could act as both. But anyone could set up as a solicitor, whereas an attorney had to have his name entered in the roll of the court before which he practised and might be struck off for misconduct. No more is known about the anonymous answerer than the little Milton tells us, but if he was indeed a serving-man turned lawyer, it would have been easier for him to have become a solicitor, and it is more likely that this alone was his proper designation. Milton may well then be ignoring the precise application of these terms.[3] In the sample from the second edition of *Doctrine and Discipline*, taken *in toto* from the added address to Parliament, Milton appeals to them variously as 'Renowned Parlament' (II, 222), 'select Assembly' (ibid.), 'Lords and Commons' (p. 224), 'Worthies in Parlament' (p. 226), and 'worthy Senators' (p. 230).

The word frequencies in Milton's tracts of 1649 reflect similar lexical preferences. Thus, in *Observations*, Milton variously terms the slanderous charges made against Parliament and its supporters in the documents under attack 'injurious words' (III, 300), 'Articles . . . full of contumely' (ibid.), 'slanderous aspersions' (ibid.), 'calumnies' (ibid., 1. 25), 'evill and reproachfull language' (p. 308), and 'a meer slander' (p. 311). Again, in the sample from *Eikonoklastes*, the masses who support the King and whom he most frequently calls 'the people' are also referred to as the 'vulgar' (III, 339. 4), 'the Common sort' (ibid.), 'that

Vulgar audience' (p. 342), and the 'multitude' (p. 345. 16).
Many such tight clusters of synonyms could be cited from the
pamphlets of 1649. All his intermediate tracts follow the pattern
of his anti-prelatical works and the practice of generally favour-
ing repetitions rather than synonyms emerges as a feature,
within the Milton canon, unique to his final tracts.

Milton's strictures on the style of *Answer to a Book* disclose a
further insight into how in the 1640s he perceived the importance
of lexical variety. The 3,000-word sample from that pamphlet
has fewer lexical items than any other from the Miltonic and
non-Miltonic tracts analysed. Within it the phrase 'put away',
meaning 'divorce', occurs 17 times, 8 times in the common
biblical locution 'put away his wife'. Close approximations to
Milton's phrase '*indisposition, unfitnes, or contrariety of mind*'
(*Doctrine*, both editions, II, 242) occur more than a dozen times.
Such repetition is plainly not to Milton's taste. He criticizes the
author witheringly, selecting for comment a later passage, a discussion of the Pauline text 'better to marry than to burn' (1 Cor.
7:9) in which he uses in consecutive pages 'burning in lust' and
'to burn in lust' six times (*Answer to a Book*, pp. 12-13). Milton
remarks:

. . . to prove that contrariety of minde is not a greater cause of divorce,
then corporal frigidity, hee enters into such a tedious and drawling tale
of *burning, and burning, and lust and burning*, that the dull argument it self
burnes to, for want of stirring; and yet all this burning is not able to
expell the frigidity of his brain (*Colasterion*, II, 740).

Evidently, Milton not only avoided lexical repetition in his own
tracts of the period but is sensitive to and deplores the trait in
others.

8. OTHER LEXICAL FEATURES

As I noted earlier, Milton forms very few words in his first and final pamphlets by direct borrowing from foreign languages, and those he does borrow often carry a distinctly critical moral weight, as though their foreignness suggests that there is something outlandish and un-English about the concepts they denote.[1] Milton's hesitancy about such borrowings and his sense of their alien quality find explicit expression in certain stylistic observations he makes in the intervenient tracts.

In a counter-thrust at Prynne, he identifies him as 'him who in his *Subitanes* hath thus censur'd' (*Colasterion*, II, 723), picking on one of his lexical eccentricities, as the Yale editor notes (ibid., n. 8). Prynne had coined 'subitane' early in his career[2] from the Latin 'subitaneus' as an alternative to the long-native 'sudden', and though it apparently found no wide currency, he persevered with it. The *OED* cites further examples from his tracts of the 1640s. For Milton, it seems, his use of a redundant word, adopted to show his own familiarity with classical tongues rather than to fill any lacuna in the English lexicon, epitomizes the vanity and affectation of his opponent.

He harries the author of *Eikon Basilike* for another classical borrowing. He quotes '*Who were the chiefe Demagogues to send for those Tumults, some alive are not ignorant,*' (it occurs on p. 17 of the edition selected for this study),[3] and picks up the neologism, criticizing 'the affrightment of this Goblin word; for the King by his leave cannot coine English as he could Money, to be current' (*Eikonoklastes*, III, 392-3). We must concede something to Joseph Jane, the would-be confuter of *Eikonoklastes*, who remarks:

And this learned observation upon the word Demagogue deserves the Laurell. Why is demagogue amore [*sic*] *hob goblin* word, then Pedagogue? . . . And why may not the King make an English word current, as well as another, There are very many whose knowne stile, and ortography is beneath the Kings, that could have transcribed Demagogue out of many English Authors without offending against ortography.[4]

Most probably, Jane errs in his clumsily worded assertion that 'demagogue' can be found in works antedating *Eikon Basilike* (if that, indeed, is what his final sentence means). The *OED* notes no earlier examples, and he may be confusing the incidence of it in works, considered below, that closely postdate *Eikon Basilike*. However, Jane is right to point to the long history of 'pedagogue' within the language. According to the *OED*, it had been in use since the fifteenth century, and Milton uses it himself (*Areopagitica*, II, 531. 24). Moreover, the first element of 'demagogue', δῆμος, was familiar enough in 'democracy', borrowed through French in the early sixteenth century. Milton's comment reveals something of the profundity of his republicanism. He seems to resent strongly the assumption that a king should prescribe how the English language should develop. But it also points to his grave reservations about the role of borrowing in the expansion of the English lexicon. Milton clearly believes in the vernacular as a medium of communication with English readers, not as a showpiece for specious erudition. However, 'demagogue' has certainly proved useful—useless borrowings do not survive. It found immediate acceptance with other contemporaries. The author of *Eikon Alethine* took it up without demur (p. 22. 14) and Hobbes quickly adopted it.[5] In the context of linguistic borrowing, Milton, ironically so often regarded as the arch-classicist, is avowedly a populist and a nationalist.

This can probably be seen best in his onslaught in *Areopagitica* on the word 'imprimatur', borrowed into English in 1640 and for which no alternative seems to have been formed out of the native resources of the language:

These [quoted examples of imprimaturs] are the prety responsories, these are the deare Antiphonies that so bewitcht of late our Prelats, and their Chaplaines with the goodly Eccho they made; and besotted us to the gay imitation of a lordly *Imprimatur*, one from Lambeth house, another from the West end of *Pauls*; so apishly Romanizing, that the word of command still was set downe in Latine; as if the learned Grammaticall pen that wrote it, would cast no ink without Latine; or perhaps, as they thought, because no vulgar tongue was worthy to express the pure conceit of an *Imprimatur*; but rather, as I hope, for that our English, the language of men ever famous, and formost in the atchievements of liberty, will not easily finde servile letters anow to spell such a dictatorie presumption English (II, 504-5).

As an attempt to give a moral framework to the study of languages, Milton's observations are plainly unconvincing. It is an easy matter to cite words formed from the native resources of English that express concepts of political and social repression and control, such as 'thraldom' or 'bondman'. However, his comments establish clearly the ethical context within which he considered linguistic issues.

It is exciting to see the application of his theoretical position in the processes he favours for his own neologizing.[6] As in the tracts considered above, in his intervenient pamphlets loan-words are infrequent in comparison with other kinds of Miltonic word-formation. As in his anti-prelatical pamphlets, Milton's borrowings here fall into two groups—words the foreignness of which suggests the outlandishness of the concepts they denote and words adopted to provide a technical terminology.[7] The former group are numerically fewer than in the earliest tracts, but there are some interesting examples. Thus, when excluding appraisal of other people's educational schemes from *Of Education*, he says, 'to search what many modern *Janua's* and *Didactics* more then ever I shall read, have projected, my inclination leads me not' (II, 364-6). The new words are taken from the titles of two Latin tracts by Comenius, *Janua Linguarum Reserata* and *Didactica Magna*. Milton's phrase has provoked some critical controversy. Masson comments, 'It is as if he had said [to Hartlib], "I know your enthusiasm for your Pansophic friend; but I have not read his books on Education, and do not mean to do so." '[8] However, Sirluck, the Yale editor, believes Milton was familiar with the *Janua* and, in manuscript form, with the *Didactica*. He would interpret this as his attempt to *avoid* rudeness to Hartlib, to whom the tract is addressed, about his friend Comenius (II, 184-216). Whatever Milton's acquaintance with these works, Masson is surely closer to assessing the tone of the passage. Yet Milton is not specifically rejecting the tracts of Comenius, but rather the considerable body of writing produced by his disciples.[9] The alien quality of the words he borrows into English connotes the bookish abstruseness and aridity of the many works he would dismiss from consideration. Similarly, when he writes of the 'polluted orts and refuse of *Arcadia's* and *Romances*' (*Eikonoklastes*, III, 364), the Latinate word '*Arcadia's*', adopted from Sidney's title, suggests something of the Mediterranean indulgence of the literary tradition with which he would have his Puritan readers most strongly associate Charles, an effect probably reinforced by the 'Roman-' element in '*Romances*'. In *Areopagitica*, after establishing the links between Catholicism and press-censorship, he observes, 'And this was the rare morsell so officiously snatcht up, and so ilfavouredly imitated by our inquisiturient Bishops, and the attendant minorites their Chaplains' (II, 506-7). His coining, 'inquisiturient', draws attention to itself by its six-syllable length and by its unusual termination; Latin words in the desiderative form were not often adopted into English. 'Esurient', perhaps now the most widely current, post-dated *Areopagitica*, and I can think of only 'parturient' in general use at the time. The adoption of a Latin suffix, rare in English, connotes, perhaps, how alien the activity of censorial investigation is to the English political tradition. The element 'inquisit-' makes a connection with a Protestant bugbear, the Inquisition. The effect is ingeniously increased by Milton's clever extension of the word 'minorites', previously a proper name of an order of friars, to mean 'person of lower rank'.[10] The word, of course, retains its taint of popery.

The majority of Milton's foreign borrowings, however, are less interesting and occur when he feels a lacuna in technical terminology. In general he takes care that comprehension is not threatened. Thus, when he writes 'yeers and good generall precepts will have furnisht them more distinctly with that act of reason which in *Ethics* is call'd *Proairesis*' (*Of Education*, II, 396), he introduces a new technical term, '*Proairesis*', in such a way as to acknowledge its newness and to refer his reader to its origin. 'Ethics' was frequently used as a brief name for Aristotle's *Nicomachean Ethics*,[11] whence, as the Yale editor notes (II, 396 n. 126), Milton adopts the new word. He takes from Greek two other technical terms—'*gnomologies*' (II, 668. 16) and '*Etymologicon*' (ibid., p. 672. 7)—in *Tetrachordon*, but the impact is softened and comprehensibility eased by the use in English since the sixteenth century of cognate words, 'gnome' and 'etymology'.[12] From Hebrew he borrows 'Keri' and 'Chetiv' (*Areo-*

pagitica, II, 517), 'technical terms of *Masorah*, the textual criticism of Hebrew Scriptures' (ibid., n. 111). Once more, he glosses them as he introduces them ('his marginall Keri' and 'the textuall Chetiv').

It is clear from the groups of pamphlets selected for comparison with the intervenient Miltonic tracts that the great age of language expansion through borrowing was over. Further, the new borrowings his contemporaries make seem of a different quality from Milton's. The adoption of foreign words to connote outlandishness does not characterize any of his contemporaries from the central groups, nor in general does the formation of technical terminology. The author of *Eikon Basilike* was singularly felicitous in his selection of loan-words. Besides introducing 'demagogue', he borrowed 'effronterie' from the French (p. 40. 26).[13] Its passage was probably eased by the sixteenth-century borrowing of 'effronted' (from *effronté*) and it found immediate acceptance. It is used by the author of *Eikon Alethine* (p. 86. 6-7). Others have proved less successful. In *Eikon Alethine* the author borrows, presumably from neo-classical treatises on logic, the terms '*Correlatum*' (p. 86. 6-7) and '*Relatum*' (ibid., 1. 7), but these have not survived, nor has the Latin loan-word 'infandum' (p. 65. 21), which seems the merest ostentation of learning in that there were several native alternatives already available. Featley fashions the curious phrase '*harsh croaking* and *coaxation*' (*Dippers Dipt*, p. 227) in an image in which he likens preaching to the noise of frogs. 'Coaxation' may well have seemed to be generated by affixation from 'coax', but is in fact a classical loan-word, duplicating 'croaking', for which it is a precise synonym. Perhaps Featley is making an oblique reference to Aristophanes' *The Frogs*—the word is formed ultimately from $Koαξ$, the word he uses to express the croaking of the chorus[14]—but it may well be mere affectation, a wanton adoption of a foreign borrowing with the additional disadvantage of confusion with a native English word.

The overwhelming majority of Miltonic neologisms from the intervenient tracts are formed from the native resources of the language by the normal processes of word-formation. Affixation is very important. Hence, he generates by suffixation 'literalism' (*Doctrine*, II, 334. 7), 'muselesse' (*Areopagitica*, II, 496. 8), 'degenerately' (*Tetrachordon*, II, 587. 3), 'desertrice' (ibid.,

p. 605. 25), '*Bonner*-like' (*Colasterion*, II, 724. 5), 'jabberment' (ibid., p. 755. 6), '*despotic*' (*Tenure*, III, 233. 13), 'motionists' (ibid., p. 255. 29), 'Preistery' (*Eikonoklastes*, III, 366. 9), and 'assassinaters' (ibid., p. 578. 4). By prefixation he forms 'counter-statute' (*Doctrine*, II, 292. 17), 'unfrocking' (*Areopagitica*, II, 550. 9), 'miswedded' (*Tetrachordon*, II, 607. 9), '*Sub advocate*' (*Colasterion*, II, 730. 25), 'unmaskuline' (*Tenure*, III, 195. 9), 'self-defence' (ibid., p. 254. 27), 'co-interest' (*Observations*, III, 334. 9) and 'Arch-Presbytery' (*Eikonoklastes*, III, 492. 22). The variety of affixes he utilizes is particularly noteworthy. Milton's readiness to form words by affixation is common to both central groups of tracts and reflects again an impatience with linguistic restrictions, an unwillingness to resort to periphrasis. Hence, he coins 'quotationists' (*Doctrine*, II, 230. 7) in preference to some phrase such as 'they who base argument on quotations'. Hence, too, 'Gospelliz'd' (ibid., p. 262. 21) instead of 'imparted according to the spirit of the Gospel'. Other techniques figure in the process of word-formation. Milton adopts an adjective as a noun—'dehortatory' (*Observations*, III, 334. 8), a noun as a verb—'padlockt' (*Colasterion*, II, 732. 8), and back-formation—'cuttling' (ibid., p. 735. 12).

Decidedly the most interesting Miltonic neologisms are formed by compounding. As in some of his anti-prelatical tracts, some compounds are effectively syncopated images. Thus, court-room debate is termed 'tongue-fence' (*Doctrine*, II, 347. 20),[15] the only heroism lawyers are capable of. Opponents among the clergy are variously 'Pulpit-firebrands', 'Church-wolves', and 'fellow-locusts' (*Tenure*, III, 243. 2, 257. 24, 258. 11). He coins for small dogs the word 'shin-barkers' (*Colasterion*, II, 757. 3) in a passage likening annoyance from his opponents to that experienced by a man hampered by curs.[16] His word points up finely the canine aspects he would see in his own annoyers— that, though they are trivial and ultimately impotent pests, they yap irritatingly around the feet of those they cannot effectively attack. Sometimes compounds startlingly juxtapose words one would not expect to find together, as in 'dinner-Doctrin' (*Eikonoklastes*, III, 530. 10). However, by no means all the neologisms formed by compounding are so ambitious—consider 'Law-witnessing' (*Doctrine*, II, 335. 6), 'Presse-corrector' (*Areopagitica*,

II, 530. 31), 'Law-beaten' (*Tetrachordon*, II, 630. 10), 'Artillery-ground' (*Tenure*, III, 255. 16), 'all-seeing' (*Eikonoklastes*, III, 362. 14).

As explained earlier, accurate quantitative comparison with lexis of selected contemporary pamphlets is precluded by the statistical problems inherent in comparing samples of different sizes and by the impossibility of extracting exhaustive lists of new coinings.[17] However, the neologisms formed by Milton's contemporaries certainly support some critical observation and help to define the status of Milton's practice in the context of the norms for the genre.

Hammond and the anonymous confuter of *Doctrine and Discipline* seem reluctant to form new words through affixation and compounding and produce a bare handful of examples between them. Canne, too, seems restrained in his coinings. Nevertheless, the authors of *Eikon Alethine* and *Eikon Basilike* and, perhaps to a lesser extent, Featley and Williams, form words quite freely from native resources. Milton clearly stands with the latter group.

As in Milton, affixation plays an important part in word formation among most contemporaries, producing, for example, 'fallaciously' (*Dippers Dipt*, p. 74. 23), 'unpoisonous' (*Eikon Basilike*, p. 222. 20), 'ungarrison'd' (*Eikon Alethine*, p. 43. 30). The most significant differences between Milton's practice and that of his contemporaries is qualitative and concerns formation through compounding. Almost all the compounds among the other pamphleteers are stylistically unexciting, very frequently the simple juxtaposition of attributive substantives with other nouns, as in '*Scripture-grounds*' (*Eikon Basilike*, p. 130. 18), '*Scripture-Canons*' (ibid., p. 133. 31), 'Court-Divinity' (*Eikon Alethine*, p. 16. 18), 'Court-priests' (ibid., p. 58. 5), 'Court-oppression' (ibid., p. 20. 21), 'Court-Doctors' (ibid., sig. K3r, p. 69. 13), 'Court-preacher' (ibid., p. 87. 29), etc. The only compound that presents an unusual juxtaposition of words is '*Sucking-Rogues*' (ibid., Epistle, sig. Alr. 22), an interesting term for petty criminals, though it is worth noting[18] that Joseph Beaumont had used the phrase 'sucking Knaves' in 1648. '*State-Archers*' (*Golden Rule*, p. 1. 9), when extracted from its context, may seem a syncopated image of the Miltonic type discussed above. However, the word occurs in a long analogy which

Canne draws between Alcon of Crete, who killed a dragon threatening his son by shooting it with an arrow, and the regicidal government, and the attributive element is merely part of the linking mechanism of the image, pointing up the area of comparison. Again, 'State-sores' (*Eikon Basilike*, p. 6. 5) is part of a larger image—'I see it a bad exchange to wound a man's conscience, thereby to salv State-sores'—rather than an abbreviated image in itself.

I concluded above[19] that Milton's lexis in his anti-prelatical and final tracts absorbed many of the words that had entered English within the forty years preceding publication. This holds true also for the intervening pamphlets, and once more by far the largest proportion of the new words have been formed from the native resources of the language by compounding and affixation, such as 'over-front' (*Doctrine*, II, 228. 16), 'divorcer' (ibid., p. 350. 2), 'uncatechis'd' (*Areopagitica*, II, 529. 16), 'argumentative' (*Tetrachordon*, II, 607. 33), 'unconverted' (*Tenure*, III, 235, 7), 'fellow-subjects' (ibid., p. 214. 14), 'undebated' (*Observations*, III, 311. 20), 'Priestlings' (ibid., p. 322. 12), 'misdevotion' (*Eikonoklastes*, III, 552. 23), 'magnanimously' (ibid., p. 580. 14). These lists, of course, are illustrative rather than exhaustive.

As with tracts previously considered, foreign loan-words remain a small, though not unimportant, part of the fairly new words that he uses. In general, they are technical terms such as '*Phaenomenon*' (*Doctrine*, II, 243. 18), '*Prutenick*' (ibid., p. 243. 20), '*Usu-fructuary*' (*Observations*, III, 306. 4), 'Granado's' (*Eikonoklastes*, III, 450. 13). The anti-prelatical tracts are distinguished by Milton's occasional manipulation of the obtrusive foreignness of certain recent loan-words, using them to connote an outlandishness much as he continues to do at times with words of his own borrowing in the intervenient tracts. However, such application of recent loan-words does not seem a significant feature of his central pamphlets.

Milton's practice of readily adopting recently formed or borrowed words is solidly in line with that of his contemporaries. Even those who are relatively reluctant to form their own neologisms adopt words that are fairly fresh to the language. Thus, Hammond uses 'commendablenesse' (*Humble Address*, p. 2. 35), 'exorbitancy' (ibid., p. 6. 14), '*populacy*' (ibid., p. 7. 2), 'irreversibly' (ibid., 9. 16), and the replier to *Doctrine and Discipline* adopts 'implicitely' (*Answer to a Book*, sig. B3v, p. 6. 26), 'promiscuously' (ibid., 23. 33), '*non compos mentis*' (ibid., p. 43. 3). Neither list is by any means exhaustive. The tracts of contemporaries abound in new political vocabulary and the vocabulary of controversial theology, such as '*Paedo-baptisme*' (*Dippers Dipt*, Epistle, sig. Clr. 8), 'Anti-Episcopal' (*Eikon Basilike*, p. 51. 18), '*Kirk-Government*' (ibid., p. 93. 30), 'Ship-money' (*Eikon Alethine*, p. 35. 11), 'Royalists' (*Golden Rule*, Epistle, sig. A2v. 12), '*Covenant-wise*' (ibid., p. 27. 30).

Milton's practice in extending the sense of words already in the language seems freer in the pamphlets of 1643 to 1645 than in those of 1649. In general, such extensions reflect an impatience with the restrictions of linguistic convention. Thus, he uses hitherto intransitive verbs transitively, such as 'degenerates' (*Tetrachordon*, II, 632. 16), or absolutely, such as 'dazl'd' (*Eikonoklastes*, III, 478. 36), or reflexively, 'amaze' (*Colasterion*, II, 736. 11); or hitherto transitive verbs intransitively, such as 'proverbing' (*Observations*, III, 333. 8). Some of his innovations, particularly in the tracts of 1643 to 1645, exhibit considerable stylistic ingenuity. Thus, in:

But if we give way to politick dispensations of lewd uncleannesse, the first good consequence of such a relaxe will be the justifying of papal stews, joyn'd with a toleration of epidemick whordom (*Doctrine*, II, 322),

he extends the meaning of 'epidemick' beyond its customary, strictly medical application to suggest how pervasive the immorality will be. His choice of words serves also obliquely to identify the evils he would combat with disease, and thus he reinforces a comparison reiterated throughout that tract between divorce and healing and between unhappy marriage and disease.[20] Again, in his objection to the '*alphabetical* servility' (ibid., p. 280) of those who would observe the letter of the law, his extension of the adjective from meaning merely 'of, pertaining to, or in order of the alphabet' (*OED* 1) to some extent connotes the clerkish inflexibility and pettiness of those he is attacking.

Among the contemporaries considered, semantic extension seems a less prominent feature, and this is, perhaps, a further indicator of Milton's greater flexibility. The author of *Mans*

Mortallitie, however, does attempt to develop a scientific or quasi-scientific terminology for his heresy through the re-application of words already in the language, such as '*conceptive*' (p. 14. 16), '*Stative*' (p. 47. 27), and '*Effluction*' (p. 48. 27).

As with the tracts considered earlier, both Miltonic and non-Miltonic pamphlets of the intervenient periods are well sprinkled with words used in senses that had only recently developed, such as 'Gnostics' (*OED* 2, *Tetrachordon*, II, 579. 3), 'accommodation' (*OED* 4, *Tenure*, III, 240. 21), 'Zelots' (*OED* 2, *Eikonoklastes*, III, 348. 24), 'Libertinisme' (*OED* 1, *Dippers Dipt*, p. 198. 25), '*Cessation*' (*OED* 1 b, *Eikon Basilike*, p. 82. 29).

The generation of unusual and exciting collocations was perhaps the most remarkable lexical feature of Milton's anti-prelatical tracts, and one which served sharply to distinguish these pamphlets not only from his last group but also from those contemporary works considered in the first section.[21] Such pyrotechnics remain prominent in his tracts of 1643 to 1645. As earlier, Milton often uses words relating to writing in environments that would normally predict something concrete or animate. Thus, in 'we may not marvell, if not so often bad, as good Books were silenc't' (*Areopagitica*, II, 500), 'Books' is collocated with a verb normally predicting an animate noun. It seems a strange notion to 'silence' something which cannot itself emit sound. He criticizes Ambrose's 'contorted sentences' (*Tetrachordon*, II, 698), though 'contort' and its participles seem generally to relate to more concrete objects than an element of prose style. Threatening to write a satirical lampoon, Milton says he may 'curle up this gliding prose into a rough *Sotadic*' (*Colasterion*, II, 757), though 'curle' in earlier contexts quoted by the *OED* had related to concrete nouns and the verb 'glide' is generally used of ships, streams, animals, or spirits. Once more, such abnormal collocations serve obliquely to suggest that literature is a concrete or living thing.

Similarly, he retains into his second period his habit of treating abstract nouns expressing the warring elements of truth and falsehood, vice and virtue, as though they, too, had concreteness or animation. 'Custome' is 'receiv'd for the best instructer' (*Doctrine*, II, 222); law is 'the exacter of our obedience' (ibid., p. 303); Milton wonders how Parliament will 'honour Truth' (*Areopagitica*, II, 507), though, it seems, in normal usage only humans and their conduct are honoured. The forces of progress and reaction are offered as contenders in some mortal struggle. Milton is making explicit a deeply held notion when he wishes, 'Let [Truth] and Falshood grapple; who ever knew Truth put to the wors, in a free and open encounter' (ibid., p. 561).

Unusual collocations become much rarer in the pamphlets of 1649. I note a handful of examples, almost all from *Eikonoklastes*. Thus, truth is 'not smother'd, but sent abroad' (*Eikonoklastes*, III, 339). Kings 'fawn upon Philosophie', which 'as well requites them' (ibid., p. 413). However, though Milton patently dislikes the style of *Eikon Basilike* and makes a number of comments on it, he does not draw upon the mechanism of abnormal collocation to express his dislike as once he might have done.

Abnormal collocations are rare in the non-Miltonic tracts, except in *The Bloudy Tenent*. This pamphlet has the format of a dialogue between the allegorical figures of 'Peace' and 'Truth'. Inevitably, the 'conversation' between these figures causes the words for the abstractions they represent to be used in lexical environments where one would expect a name, as in 'Begin (sweet *Peace*) read and propound' (p. 118) or 'Deare *Truth*, you have showne me a little draught' (p. 201). Outside such formal requirements of his allegory, Williams shows no particular enthusiasm for generating unusual collocations.

In general, then, Milton's lexis in the tracts of 1643 to 1645 and 1649 retains the high degree of creativity and innovation that distinguished his earliest pamphlets from his final group and from those of his contemporaries, though some features exhibit a degree of levelling down in 1649.

9. SYNTAX

A comparison of Milton's first and final tracts disclosed only two aspects of syntax which differed between the groups, the incidence and positioning of adjectives. To establish when these shifts occurred I analysed 3,000-word samples taken from the beginning of each of his tracts of 1643 to 1645 and 1649 (together with samples from selected contemporary pamphlets). Once more, I worked from key-word-in-context concordances generated by COCOA. (I found no significant differences between the two editions of *Doctrine and Discipline*, and so present figures drawn only from the second.)

TABLE 19

Incidence of adjectives in intervenient groups (expressed as percentage of all words in samples)

	%
Miltonic: 1643-5	
Doctrine	8.0
Of Education	8.6
Areopagitica	5.9
Tetrachordon	7.0
Colasterion	5.8
Miltonic: 1649	
Tenure	6.7
Observations	6.8
Eikonoklastes	6.3
Non-Miltonic: 1643-5	
Answer to a Book	2.4
Bloudy Tenent	6.3
Dippers Dipt	5.7
Mans Mortallitie	5.0
Non-Miltonic: 1649	
Eikon Alethine	5.5
Eikon Basilike	4.6
Golden Rule	4.3
Humble Address	3.8

In Milton's anti-prelatical tracts adjectives constituted between 6.0 and 8.5 per cent of all the words in the samples, whereas in the later tracts, except for the atavistic *Readie and Easie Way* and the much later *Of True Religion*, the range was lower, between 5.2 and 5.5 per cent of all the words in the samples.[1] His practice for the intervenient groups is set out in Table 19. All but two of Milton's tracts fall within the range of his practice in the anti-prelatical pamphlets, and these, *Areopagitica* and *Colasterion*, do not fall far short. I noted earlier that Milton uses relatively quite a lot of adjectives. Among the tracts considered earlier, only four contemporaries penetrated the range defined by his tracts. Again, in the intervenient tracts, only one writer, Roger Williams, uses as many adjectives as Milton.

Between 6.8 and 9.5 per cent of adjectives in Milton's final tracts are placed in positions (other than in predication) after the

TABLE 20

Positioning of adjectives in intervenient groups
(expressed as percentage of all adjectives in samples)

	Before noun %	After noun %	Predi- cated %	Other %
Miltonic: 1643-5				
Doctrine	84.6	5.8	8.3	1.2
Of Education	80.2	9.7	9.7	0.4
Areopagitica	77.3	4.0	15.9	2.8
Tetrachordon	75.8	4.7	16.6	2.8
Colasterion	74.8	5.1	18.9	1.1
Miltonic: 1649				
Tenure	71.5	4.0	20.0	4.5
Observations	76.8	9.6	12.8	0.5
Eikonoklastes	74.1	11.6	11.6	2.6
Non-Miltonic: 1643-5				
Answer to a Book	54.9	4.2	38.0	2.8
Bloudy Tenent	79.3	5.3	10.6	4.8
Dippers Dipt	83.0	4.7	9.4	2.9
Mans Mortallitie	46.3	5.4	29.5	18.8
Non-Miltonic: 1649				
Eikon Alethine	75.9	4.8	16.9	2.4
Eikon Basilike	74.8	1.4	23.0	0.7
Golden Rule	70.7	6.2	18.5	4.6
Humble Address	75.4	1.6	17.5	5.3

nouns to which they refer.[2] High incidence of postponement
occurred in two of Milton's anti-prelatical tracts, but it is not
generally a feature of his contemporaries. It is clear from Table
20 that, though high incidence of postonement occurs in some
intervenient Miltonic pamphlets, it is not a persistent feature as
in his last tracts. It seems an unusual phenomenon in mid-
century polemical prose.

I had approached analysis of Milton's prose expecting to find,
as others had done, that his syntax contributes very largely to
distinguishing its texture. After all, this is what generally strikes
the uninformed modern reader as most distinctive about his
style. However, my study has invalidated the usual preconcep-
tions. Seen in the context of contemporary norms for the genre,
Milton's syntax is relatively unremarkable, and, except for two
shifts in his use of adjectives, it does not develop during his
career.

My findings in this and the corresponding chapter in the first
section are thin, and may well seem both unexciting and a poor
return on the effort invested in their acquisition. But in their
negative and limited nature lies their considerable significance
for Milton studies. How distorted our perception of his prose
had been by our inadequate and incorrect stylistic expectations!
Placed in the appropriate context, what had once appeared so
eccentric seems relatively unimportant, and we can recognize
and recapture the genuine genius of his prose.

10. IMAGERY

I established that the density of imagery in Milton's anti-prelatical tracts differs considerably from his practice in his last pamphlets.[1] In the former, incidence of imagery ranges from 5.3 to 8.8 images (vehicles) per thousand words. The last group have between 2.6 and 3.0 images per thousand words, except for *Readie and Easie Way*, the stylistic regression of which may be interpreted as Milton's attempt to recapture something of the spirit that inspired the early years of the Revolution.[2] Table 21 shows his practice in the remaining tracts.

TABLE 21

Incidence of imagery (including biblical imagery) in intervenient Miltonic groups (expressed as number of images (vehicles) per thousand words of text)

Miltonic: 1643-5	
Doctrine (1st edn.)	3.2
Doctrine (2nd edn.)	4.8
Of Education	1.3
Areopagitica	6.9
Tetrachordon	2.5
Colasterion	4.2
Miltonic: 1649	
Tenure	3.6
Observations	2.2
Eikonoklastes	3.0

The incidence of imagery within the 1643 to 1645 tracts varies curiously. *Areopagitica* has the same image density as his first tracts and *Colasterion* and the second edition of *Doctrine and Discipline* do not fall far short of that range. (For the first time in this study, it was possible to distinguish between the style of the two earliest editions of his first divorce tract.) However, his practice in the first edition of the *Doctrine and Discipline* and in *Tetrachordon* is more like the norm of his final pamphlets and *Of Education* in this respect is the leanest of his tracts.

The wide variation cannot be accounted for in formal terms. Indeed, *Areopagitica* is 'a Speech . . . To the Parliament of England' (title-page, II, 485) and seems to show the stylistic pyrotechnics perhaps appropriate to oral delivery. Again, the lack of flamboyance in *Of Education* may seem a consequence of its epistolary format. However, such an analysis is frustrated by the high incidence of imagery in the epistle inserted as a preface to the second edition of *Doctrine and Discipline* (II, 222-33), which has over thirty images in six pages of the original quarto. Nor can it account for the disparities between *Colasterion* and *Tetrachordon*. There is good reason to suppose that Milton regarded them as a matched, or rather complementary, pair. They appeared simultaneously. Both have titles that are Greek and metaphorical. Parker identifies them[3] as the 'twin-born progeny' alluded to in:

I did but prompt the age to quit their clogs
　　By the known rules of ancient liberty,
　　When straight a barbarous noise environs me
　　Of owls and cuckoos, asses, apes and dogs.
As when those hinds that were transformed to frogs
　　Railed at Latona's twin-born progeny
　　Which after held the sun and moon in fee.[4]

The singlar appropriateness of the image to the two tracts lends considerable weight to Parker's argument, which in turn suggests how similarly they were regarded by Milton. He would have liked the association of the uncarnal arguments of *Tetrachordon* with the sexual purity represented by Diana and the conception of the *Sol Iustitiae* presiding over *Colasterion*, the place of punishment. Clearly, their similarity in form and in the way in which Milton perceived them excludes formal considerations as explanation of the radically different image density of such 'twins'.

A subtler and more tenable interpretation is suggested by Milton's note in *Of Education* on the place of stylistic variety in rhetoric. With tantalizing brevity he writes:

And now lastly will be the time to read with them [the students of his proposed academy] those organic arts which inable men to discourse and write perspicuously, elegantly, and according to the fitted stile of lofty, mean, or lowly (II, 401).

It would have been helpful had he gone on to explain what he understood to be the characteristics of each style and the circumstances which determine which should be adopted. As it stands, the statement is, as the Yale editor notes (pp. 401-2 n. 163), just a commonplace of the classical rhetoricians. He would have known this injunction since his school-days[5] and most probably would have conceded its at least theoretical validity at any stage of his writing career. In practice, however, his anti-prelatical pamphlets manifest a considerable degree of stylistic homogeneity, even though they treat a variety of material in a number of ways. For example, *Prelatical Episcopacy* and *Church-Government* are attempts to consider what structure the Church ought to have in the light of biblical evidence and the early history of Christianity. In them Milton cites, argues from, and evaluates evidence. Yet the image density there scarcely differs from that of his vituperative, indignant *Apology*, which in purpose, material, and dialectic is quite different.

In the pamphlets of 1643 to 1645 he seems to be experimenting with the fine adjustment of texture to tone and method. *Areopagitica*, like *Of Reformation* largely a historical rhapsody, is as charged with imagery as the anti-prelatical tract, but *Of Education*, a statement, indeed almost a mere list, of his proposals, is stripped to the bone. Again, the marked contrast in his practice in the carefully exegetical *Tetrachordon*, which he himself terms 'woven close, both matter, form and style',[6] and the savage *Colasterion* shows Milton's new concern with fitting style and argument.

The changes between the two editions of the *Doctrine and Discipline* reflect Milton's initial hesitancy and perhaps confusion about the validity of adopting a plainer style for some contexts. The first edition, though not as lean as *Tetrachordon*, marks a decided falling off in image density from any English prose polemic he had written before. However, he seems to have regretted the stylistic decision. Perhaps an unsympathetic public response suggested a more vigorous exposition was called for.[7] Whatever

his motives, he certainly tries to bring the second edition into line
with his earlier tracts by the addition of material supercharged
with imagery. Some of the additions are so larded with imagery
that it is hard to understand their plain sense. Milton's literary
control slips badly as image ramps over image. In some parts of
the new prefatory epistle almost every sentence has an image,
and sometimes the imagery is perplexingly repetitive as the same
vehicle is reworked and reapplied. He writes of:

. . . Error and Custome: Who with the numerous and vulgar train
their followers, make it their chiefe designe to envie and cry-down the
industry of free reasoning, under the terms of humor, and innovation;
as if the womb of teeming Truth were to be clos'd up, if shee presume to
bring forth ought, that sorts not with their unchew'd notions and sup-
positions (II, 224),

and, on the same page (in the original):

For Truth is as impossible to be soil'd by any outward touch, as the Sun
beam. Though this ill hap wait on her nativity, that shee never comes
into the world, but like a Bastard, to the ignominy of him that brought
him forth: till Time the Midwife rather then the mother of Truth, have
washt and salted the Infant, declar'd her legitimat, and Churcht the
father of his young *Minerva*, from the needlesse causes of his purgation
(ibid., p. 225).

Truth, which we had been invited to conceptualize as a woman
in labour, must now be imagined as a newly delivered child.
Thus, the same complex image is reapplied to a reorganized
tenor in which Truth has become the object rather than the subject of parturition. The result demands an impossible athleticism
from the reader's imagination. The second quotation also shows
how Milton crams imagery into the material he has added. The
reference to childbirth follows hard upon an undeveloped
comparison of Truth and sunshine and modulates into a literary
grotesque which, as the Yale editor notes (p. 225 n. 20), mingles
classical myth with the Anglican service of churching women
after childbirth.

The *Tenure*, which is the most theoretical of the tracts of 1649
and like *Areopagitica* and *Of Reformation*, depends heavily on the
morally charged reworking of history, does have quite a high

image density, though it falls a good deal short of previous pamphlets utilizing this dialectical method. The tracts which Milton was authorized to write against Ormond's treaty with the Irish rebels and against *Eikon Basilike*, *Observations*, and *Eikonoklastes*, show the same reduction in density as the plainer tracts of the 1643 to 1645 group and anticipate the normal style of his immediately pre-Restoration writings.

Milton's practice in the pamphlets of 1649, and especially *Eikonoklastes*, is more remarkable if seen in comparison with *Eikon Basilike* itself and *Eikon Alethine*, the other point-by-point refutation it provoked. As Table 22 shows, the incidence of imagery in five of the non-Miltonic tracts of 1643 to 1645 and 1649 is no higher than in Milton's 1649 pamphlets. However,

TABLE 22

Incidence of imagery (including biblical imagery) on intervenient non-Miltonic groups (expressed as numbers of images (vehicles) per thousand words of text)

Non-Miltonic: 1643-5	
Answer to a Book	0.7
Bloudy Tenent	4.5
Dippers Dipt	2.6
Mans Mortallitie	2.7
Non-Miltonic: 1649	
Eikon Alethine	6.8
Eikon Basilike	4.9
Golden Rule	2.1
Humble Address	0.9

the author of *Eikon Basilike* uses a considerable amount, not only in the inset prayers but in his exposition and analysis of events. The first detailed reply to it, the ingenious and rather devious *Eikon Alethine*, attempts a colourful response both in its general approach and the texture of the prose. The author argues that *Eikon Basilike* is clearly a forgery that discredits the king, so an accurate account is called for, which in turn, of course, vindicates the actions of Parliament. Apparent sympathy for Charles's reputation is the author's springboard into his regicide apology. Besides this polemical subtlety, he tries to outshine his target stylistically. Although the character of his imagery differs in several ways from that of *Eikon Basilike*, its density is part of this attempt to rival it in stylistic liveliness. It contrasts starkly with Milton's own response to what the anonymous author calls the 'painted grapes' and *'giganticke garbe of pace and language'* (*Eikon Alethine*, Epistle, sig. A3v) of the king's book. Previously, when directly attacking another tract, Milton had used a higher density of imagery than his opponent. Yet his response to the flashiness of *Eikon Basilike* is a sober refutation in the new leaner style. He refuses to deviate from what had become in the earlier tracts of 1649 his standard practice.

   In the earlier comparison of the non-biblical imagery of the first and final pamphlets I noted that the simple-substitution structure (that is, images in which one metaphorical term replaces a term in the tenor) was in the anti-prelatical tracts decidedly less common than extended-substitution imagery (that is, imagery in which the metaphor extends beyond one element of the tenor). This is not the case in the last group of Miltonic tracts (except for the very short *Brief Notes*).[8] Table 23 presents information on this feature in the intervening pamphlets. Of course, in some tracts the groups of such images are quite small. Nevertheless, though less distinctly than with the study of image density, a pattern emerges that suggests a certain experimentation in the 1643 to 1645 pamphlets and in 1649 a movement towards the simplicity of his final tracts. As argued earlier, simple substitution, in its plainness, characterizes the

TABLE 23

Extended-substitution imagery expressed as a
proportion of simple-substitution imagery in intervenient
Miltonic groups (extended substitutions ÷ simple substitutions)

Miltonic: 1643-5	
Doctrine (1st edn.)	0.9
Doctrine (2nd edn.)	1.2
Of Education	1.7
Areopagitica	2.0
Tetrachordon	1.1
Colasterion	2.3
Miltonic: 1649	
Tenure	1.1
Observations	1.3
Eikonoklastes	0.9

prose as a medium suitable for the transmission of fact and argument, whereas extended-substitution imagery often makes the argument less immediately comprehensible.

In *Tetrachordon* and, to a lesser extent, in *Of Education* he does not develop imagery into extended substitutions as often as he does in *Areopagitica* and *Colasterion*. He is less willing to disrupt his exposition of fact and argument with the sort of imagery he so warmly favoured in his first tracts. His additions to *Doctrine and Discipline* shift slightly its stylistic balance in the direction of the more vivid pamphlets of the group, though less decisively than with the shift in image density. He does once add to a simple substitution, though in one of his duller metaphors, extending 'to make sin it self a free Citizen of the Commonwealth' to 'to make sin it self, the ever alien & vassal sin, a free Citizen of the Commonwealth' (II, 286). All three tracts of 1649 show the predilections of his last group.

Once more, Milton's practice in the 1649 tracts seems the more remarkable in the context of the other contributions to the regicide debate. The relative incidence of simple and extended imagery in the pamphlets of the non-Miltonic group is recorded in Table 24. John Canne has a taste for anecdotal (and thus, of

TABLE 24

Extended-substitution imagery expressed as a proportion of simple-substitution imagery in intervenient non-Miltonic groups (extended substitutions: ÷ simple substitutions)

Non-Miltonic: 1643-5	
Answer to a Book	1.0
Bloudy Tenent	2.8
Dippers Dipt	4.3
Mans Mortallitie	0.6
Non-Miltonic: 1649	
Eikon Alethine	2.6
Eikon Basilike	2.6
Golden Rule	2.7
Humble Address	—

necessity, extended) imagery. *Eikon Basilike* has a preponderance of extended substitutions, and the author of *Eikon Alethine* equals his adversary. It is eloquent evidence of Milton's stylistic autonomy that in *Eikonoklastes* he does not deviate from the chosen style of the first two 1649 to ape or answer in kind the object of his refutation. Among the 1643 to 1645 group, Featley shows a great enthusiasm for extended substitutions, and Williams, too, uses a lot.

There are other changes in Milton's practice which are less susceptible to quantification. Some of his own comments point to a shift in his concept of what is desirable and permissible in prose. In *Church-Government*, before a most elaborate image of the chariot of zeal riding over the necks of the prelates, he introduces the aside ('that I may have leave to soare a while as the Poets use') (I, 900). He acknowledges the image that follows may be more the sort encountered in poetry but believes its inclusion in his treatise is justifiable. The author of *Eikon Basilike* uses the following image:

With what unwillingness I with-drew from *Westminster* let them judg who, unprovided of tackling and victual, are forced to Sea by a storm: yet better do so, then venture splitting or sinking on a Lee shore (p. 29).

This has certain characteristics familiar from the imagery of Milton's anti-prelatical tracts. It is multi-referential. A complex series of events and their causes are alluded to within the single analogy—the nature of the political upheaval ('a storm'), Charles's pessimism about the course adopted, and his lack of alternatives. Again , there are details ('tackling and victual') for which precise correlations in the tenor are not easily found. But now Milton tartly comments:

The Simily wherwith he begins I was about to have found fault with, as in a garb somwhat more Poetical then for a Statist: but meeting with many straines of like dress in other of his Essaies, and hearing him reported a more diligent reader of Poets, then of Politicians, I begun to think that the whole Book might perhaps be intended a peece of Poetrie (*Eikonoklastes*, III, 406).

Of course, he picks up anything with which he can beat Charles, and this point relates tacitly to his charge of plagiarism and blasphemous indecorum over the Pamela prayer, another example of his reading the wrong sort of books.[9] However, analysis of Milton's practice in 1649 strongly suggests that this declared abhorrence of 'poetic' imagery in prose polemic was sincerely felt and in accord with a major shift in his own prose style.

Those characteristics which distinguish the imagery of Milton's earliest tracts from his last—a narrative or dramatic quality, detail and description introduced into the vehicle that do not relate to elements in the tenor, and the elaboration of vehicles to cover a number of points in a complex tenor—recur, though not so frequently, in the pamphlets of 1643 to 1645. They are no less a feature of the fuller imagery used in *Tetrachordon* and *Of Education* than in the others. But such imagery has almost disappeared by 1649.

Quite often in the 1643 to 1645 pamphlets Milton relates a brief anecdote to establish the vehicle. Thus, he recounts the elaborate myth of Love's search for Anteros, the deceptions of impostors and his ultimate regeneration when he finds his 'genuin brother' (*Doctrine*, second edition only, II, 254-6). The nature of the story and the recondite neoplatonic cosmos within which it operates resemble the plot and conceptual framework of *Comus*. Again, the fate of truth is likened in another complex restatement of ancient myth to the misfortune of Osiris:

Truth indeed came once into the world with her divine Master, and was a perfect shape most glorious to look on: but when he ascended, and his Apostles after him were laid asleep, then strait arose a wicked race of deceivers, who as that story goes of the *AEgyptian Typhon* with his conspirators, how they dealt with the good *Osiris*, took the virgin Truth, hewd her lovely form into a thousand peeces, and scatter'd them to the four winds. From that time ever since, the sad friends of Truth, such as durst appear, imitating the carefull search that *Isis* made for the mangl'd body of *Osiris*, went up and down gathering up limb by limb still as they could find them. We have not yet found them all, Lords and Commons, nor ever shall doe, till her Masters second comming; he shall bring together every joynt and member, and shall mould them into an immortall feature of lovelines and perfection (*Areopagitica*, II, 549).

Note how Milton makes concrete the elements of the story. He emphasizes the physical appearance of Truth-Osiris—the 'lovely form', 'mangl'd body', and 'immortall feature'—and the violence of the assault—the body 'hewd . . . to a thousand peeces' so that it must be reconstructed 'limb by limb' and 'joynt

and member'. 'Truth' is an abstract term for 'truths', things
that are in themselves intellectual abstractions. Yet Milton
describes its abuse in a savage anecdote of considerable visual
vividness.

Occasionally, the interest may be dramatic rather than narrative, as in:

Sometimes 5 *Imprimaturs* are seen together dialogue-wise in the Piatza
of one Title page, complementing and ducking each to other with their
shav'n reverences, whether the Author, who stands by in perplexity at
the foot of his Epistle, shall to the Presse or to the spunge (ibid., p. 504).

Here is the set and the personae—a piazza and demon
priests—for an Italianate drama of Machiavellian iniquity and
the evil exercise of corruptly acquired power. Milton establishes
the backdrop and offers stage directions—'ducking' pates.
Though 'dialogue' could also be applied to non-dramatic
speech, it had by the mid-seventeenth century acquired its
modern sense of conversation written for or used by actors on a
stage.[10] Milton's selection of 'dialogue-wise' rather than, for
example, 'talking together' or 'in conversation' underscores the
dramatic nature of the image.

As in the anti-prelatical tracts, the longer imagery of the
pamphlets of 1643 to 1645 is characterized by complex vehicles
in which Milton establishes a number of referents to elements in
the tenor. Thus, for example, in:

. . . they must proceed by the steddy pace of learning onward, as at
convenient times for memories sake to retire back into the middle
ward, and sometimes into the rear of what they have been taught, untill
they have confirm'd, and solidly united the whole body of their per-
fected knowledge, like the last embattelling of a Romane legion (*Of
Education*, II, 406-7).

Milton outlines a complete programme for regulating the learning process within one technical military image.

Sometimes in his more complex imagery he extends the area
of reference to make oblique, almost subliminal, suggestions
about the tenor, as in:

We cannot therefore alwayes be contemplative or pragmaticall abroad, but have need of som delightfull intermissions, wherein the enlarg'd soul may leav off a while her severe schooling; and like a glad youth in wandring vacancy, may keep her hollidaies to joy and harmles pastime: which as she cannot well doe without company, so in no company so well as where the different sexe in most resembling unlikenes, and most unlike resemblance cannot but please best and be pleas'd in the aptitude of that variety (*Tetrachordon*, II, 597).

Central to Milton's argument on divorce is his belief that marriage is more a social than a sexual institution and that a spouse who does not provide companionship and solace should be divorced as much as one who is sexually incapable. In this passage he argues that the most committed warfaring Christian needs certain holidays and pastimes and that marriage provides such a relaxation. By selecting a schoolboy as vehicle he manages to talk about companionship in completely non-sexual terms. Why the relationship he advocates should be heterosexual is fudged over in a curiously un-Miltonic quibble ('in most resembling unlikenes, and most unlike resemblance'), which in others he might have censured as 'a Game of Tictack with words' (*Eikonoklastes*, III, 564). Milton makes a double thrust at his argument, pointing up the social implications of marriage and relegating the sexual element from consideration.

As in the anti-prelatical tracts, the vehicles in the pamphlets of 1643 to 1645 are often rich in detail which cannot be related to precise referents in the tenors. In

. . . the incredible losse, and detriment that this plot of licencing puts us to, more then if som enemy at sea should stop up all our hav'ns and ports, and creeks, it hinders and retards the importation of our richest Marchandize, Truth . . . (*Areopagitica*, II, 548),

'hav'ns and ports, and creeks' do not refer to particular faculties by which we apprehend truth. Nor are we to recognize specific opponents in his complaint that the man who publishes is 'infested, sometimes at his face, with dorrs and horsflies, somtimes beneath, with bauling whippets, and shin-barkers' set on by clergy and licencers (*Colasterion*, II, 757).

Though Milton's imagery of 1649 is not as austere as that of his final tracts, many of the characteristics of the earliest pam-

phlets which survived into 1643 to 1645 have all but disappeared. There is a solitary anecdotal image, his account of
drilling and counter-marching presbyterian divines in the *Tenure*
(III, 255-6). In general, even the imagery of the extended-
substitution type has such terseness as 'he thinks to scape that
Sea of innocent blood wherein his own guilt inevitably hath
plung'd him all over' (*Eikonoklastes*, III, 376). It is useful to contrast the vivid account of the journeying of the bird-like soul in *Of
Reformation* (I, 522)[11] with:

. . . the prayer also having less intercours and sympathy with a heart
wherin it was not conceav'd, saves it self the labour of so long a
journey downward [that is, to the heart], and flying up in hast on the
specious wings of formalitie, if it fall not back again headlong, in stead
of a prayer which was expected, presents God with a set of stale and
empty words (*Eikonoklastes*, III, 507).

There is no attempt to establish the image of the bird vividly in
the imagination of the reader. The flight described bears little
relation to the behaviour of birds, which generally do not col-
lapse to earth in mid-ascent. Milton transfers the epithet
'specious' from 'formalitie' to 'wings', further ensuring that the
analogy never escapes from the ligatures binding it to its refer-
ent, nor does he attempt to extend the vehicle to further elements
in the tenor, as he could easily have done.

His more complex imagery in the tracts of 1649 usually has a
highly schematic quality, as in his reply to prognostications of
the evils consequent upon regicide:

He bodes *much horror and bad influence after his ecclips*. He speaks his
wishes: But they who by weighing prudently things past, foresee things
to come, the best Divination, may hope rather all good successes and
happiness by removing that darkness which the mistie cloud of his
prerogative made between us and a peacefull Reformation, which is
our true Sun light, and not he, though he would be tak'n for our sun it
self (ibid., p. 455).

The material of the vehicle is patterned and organized to fit the
structure of the tenor, rather than selected because its own
organic structure inherently patterns that of the tenor. What,
after all, is 'true', as distinct from 'false' sunlight?

Among the non-Miltonic writers some attempt the type of imagery that marks his pre-1649 prose. An example of the more ambitious imagery of *Eikon Basilike* has been cited and considered earlier.[12] Images like that are quite common there, though the author does not attempt longer anecdote. Most of the extended-substitution imagery of *Eikon Alethine* is quite plain. Thus, 'how the *Delphian* spirit indited this oraculous protestation with his accustomed loop-hole to escape through, when truth shall contradict the plain sense of the words' (p. 53) typifies his practice. The image of the Delphic oracle as an analogy to the deceit of his opponent is not pursued, nor does the 'loop-hole', the method of escape, receive qualification. This apologist for regicide only once indulges in very elaborate imagery, in a series of linked references to Strafford as a rising and setting sun (pp. 9—11). Although he draws several images from classical mythology—the stories of Gyges' ring (p. 41), Oedipus and the Sphinx (p. 56), Hercules and the Hydra (p. 58), and the labyrinth of Minos (p. 90)—he never develops a powerful narrative interest in the myths themselves.

Out of the sample Featley and Canne most favour anecdotal imagery. The former takes a lot of his vehicles from the more bizarre accounts in travellers' tales and natural science, and the oddity he describes, generally in analogy with some unwholesome practice of Anabaptists, is often allowed an autonomous anecdotal interest. See, for example, his analogies between the proselytizing of Anabaptists and 'the manner of taking Apes in the *Indies*' (*Dippers Dipt*, p. 198), the mixing of errors and procreation among African fauna (p. 30) and baptism and Varro's account of sheep-dipping in Boeotia (p. 37). Sometimes such images are applied with considerable ingenuity to hit a number of referents. Featley cleverly applies his final image, an account of silencing frogs by burning a light on the bank of their pond (p. 227), to define both the nature of his opponents and the desired impact of his tract. Again, John Canne draws a fair proportion of his imagery from classical history and mythology, sometimes narrating the source material at some length and in such a way as to demonstrate its peculiar appropriateness, as in:

It is reported of one *Licas* and *Thrasilius*, being cured by Physitians of the Phrensie and phantastical conceits, grew afterwards very angry with their friends because they left them not alone in their former foolish condition. I know there is little thanks to be expected from the Kings of the earth, by seeking to remove that *State-destroying principle* which their Court-flatterers have put into them . . . (*Golden Rule*, p. 29).

Though neither Canne nor Featley matches the eloquence and polish of Milton's inset narrative, their imagery at times has both wit and liveliness. Elaboration in imagery is not a significant feature of any of the remaining non-Miltonic tracts. The change in Milton's practice in 1649 on the evidence of those contemporaries analysed cannot be attributed to any general shift in the norms of the genre.

   Imagery drawn from the Bible remains an important element in the intervenient tracts of Milton and those of his contemporaries selected for comparison. As in the tracts considered earlier, there is no clear pattern in its incidence.[13] In Milton it constitutes between 12 per cent (in *Colasterion*) and 45 per cent (in *Eikonoklastes*) of all imagery. I note no biblical imagery in *Answer to a Book*, but in the other contemporary tracts its incidence varies between 16 per cent (in *Eikon Alethine*) and 63 per cent (in *Humble Address*) of all imagery.

   Milton in some of his last group of tracts developed a practice of citing the chapter and verse of the source of his biblical imagery.[14] This occurred very infrequently earlier, and it is rare in the intervening pamphlets. He cites chapter and verse once in *Tetrachordon* (II, 587), and again in *Observations* (III, 322-3), though that is part of discussion and re-application of an image in the book he is attacking. He gives chapter reference alone in *Doctrine and Discipline* (second edition only, II, 288) and twice again in *Eikonoklastes* (III, 598, 599). Elsewhere borrowing is tacit or he uses a vaguer phrase of attribution—'the saying of St. *Peter* at the   Councell of *Jerusalem*' (*Doctrine*, II, 278), 'as the Spouse of Christ thought' (ibid., p. 251)—an allusion to the Song of Solomon, 'denounc'd by our Saviour' (*Eikonoklastes*, III, 374). Only a handful of such phrases occur.

   In most contemporaries allusion is tacit. Canne cites chapter and verse once (*Golden Rule*, p. 1), the author of *Eikon Alethine* twice (pp. 5, 96). 'R.O.' four times cites the source of images (*Mans Mortallitie*, p. 6 (twice), sig. E1r, sig. E4r), that is, in 22 per cent of his biblical imagery, and Roger Williams cites chapter and verse in 54 examples of biblical imagery, that is, in 25 per cent of all vehicles drawn from the Bible. These two alone approach the practice of Milton in his last tracts. In general, however, there appears no widely felt scruple about citation of sacred sources.

I noted above[15] that, whereas in the anti-prelatical tracts Milton tailored or abridged biblical borrowings to fit his imagery, later he often quoted exactly, even though this sometimes produced some stylistic clumsiness. This punctilious regard for the text of the most current translation, the Authorized Version, characterizes biblical imagery in neither the pamphlets of 1643 to 1645 nor those of 1649. Exact quotation rarely exceeds a brief phrase, as in 'yet God in that unapocryphal vision, said without exception, Rise *Peter*, kill and eat' (*Areopagitica*, II, 512), extracted from 'Acts 10:13, And there came a voice to him, Rise, Peter; kill and eat.' Elsewhere, Milton adjusts tenses to fit the quotation into the fabric of his prose. Thus, 'Issachar is a strong ass couching down between two burdens' (Gen. 49:14) becomes '. . . for he thought his kingdom to be *Issachar a strong Ass* that would have *couch'd downe betweene two burd'ns*, the one prelatical superstition, the other of civil tyrannie' (*Eikonoklastes*, III, 446). Again:

Song 8:6, Set me as a seal upon thine heart, as a seal upon thine arm; for love is strong as death, jealousy is cruel as the grave; its coals are coals of fire, which hath a most vehement flame.

7, Many waters cannot quench love, neither can all the floods drown it. If a man would give all the substance of his house for love, it would utterly be contemned,

is condensed to '. . . desire of joyning to it self in conjugall fellowship a fit conversing soul . . . *is stronger than death*, as the Spouse of Christ thought, *many waters cannot quench it, neither can the flouds drown it*' (*Doctrine*, II, 251). Note the discrepancy ('as strong as death' becoming 'stronger than death') introduced in the process.

The non-Miltonic writers reveal no general scruple about observing the minutiae of sacred text, so far as I can ascertain. Only two follow the Authorized Version for more than the odd phrase, the author of *Eikon Basilike*, in 7 per cent of whose biblical imagery there is substantial accurate quotation, and 'R.O.' (18 per cent).

In the anti-prelatical tracts Milton very frequently 'improved' upon material drawn from the Bible by adding detail or strengthening its narrative or dramatic quality. He rarely adds, however slightly, to the biblical vehicles of his final pamphlets.[16] Table 25 presents information about his practice in the intervening tracts and that of his contemporaries analysed. There

TABLE 25

'Improved' vehicles in intervenient groups
(expressed as percentage of all biblical imagery)

	%
Miltonic: 1643-5	
Doctrine (1st edn.)	47
Doctrine (2nd edn.)	39
Of Education	100
Areopagitica	47
Tetrachordon	48
Colasterion	67
Miltonic: 1649	
Tenure	33
Observations	11
Eikonoklastes	49
Non-Miltonic: 1643-5	
Answer to a Book	—
Bloudy Tenent	39
Dippers Dipt	33
Mans Mortallitie	11
Non-Miltonic: 1649	
Eikon Alethine	54
Eikon Basilike	29
Golden Rule	38
Humble Address	—

seems no marked falling off in the two Miltonic groups except for the fewness of improvements in the biblical imagery of his short *Observations*. The other writers introduce some non-biblical material into their imagery drawn from sacred sources, except for Hammond, who uses little imagery at all. It is perhaps worth remarking upon the formal similarities between the biblical imagery of 'R.O.' and that of Milton's final tracts. Not only is he restrained in his introduction of improvements, but also he has a greater propensity for quotation and, except for Williams, for citation, than the others or than Milton in his first three periods. 'R.O.', with the possible exception of Williams, politically and theologically the most radical of the contemporary pamphleteers considered in this study, and Milton in the twilight of the Republic share certain elements in their approach to the manipulation of the sacred text.

Quantification conceals important differences in the improvements Milton makes in the tracts of 1643 to 1645 and in those of 1649, and between his and the innovations made by his contemporaries. Sometimes in the 1643 to 1645 group Milton introduces a comic strain. From Jeremiah's 'Can the Ethiopian change his skin, or the leopard his spots? (Jer. 13:23), he creates an amusing image for the attempted conversion of a spouse, 'till he try all due means, and set some reasonable time to himselfe after which he may give over washing an Ethiope' (*Doctrine*, second edition only, II, 267). Again, alterations may improve the narrative or dramatic quality of the image. From Paul's injunction, 'Know ye not that they which run in a race run all, but one receiveth the prize? So run, that ye may obtain' (I Cor. 9:24) and probably James's 'Blessed is the man that endureth temptation: for when he is tried, he shall receive the crown of life' (Jas. 1:12) he builds:

I cannot praise a fugitive and cloister'd vertue, unexercis'd & unbreath'd, that never sallies out and sees her adversary, but slinks out of the race, where the immortal garland is to be run for, not without dust and heat (*Areopagitica*, II, 515).

Out of the plain statements of the original Milton generates an account of a pusillanimous athlete withdrawing from a fully realized competition. He points up the antithesis of the value of the prize and the 'dust and heat' by which it is attained and introduces moral evaluation through the opprobrious verb 'slink'.

In general his 'improvements' on the vehicles of biblical origin in the 1649 tracts are relatively unexciting. For example, the 'tares' of the parable of the weeds among the corn (Matt. 13:24-5) become 'Malignant Tares' (*Eikonoklastes*, III, 549),

'Diana of the Ephesians' (Acts 19:28) becomes 'his old *Ephesian Goddess*' (ibid., p. 571), and Christ's injunction 'Feed my sheep' (John 21:16) is recast into the curiously flaccid and wordy 'that [the job of bishops] being an ordinarie, fixt, & particular charge, the continual inspection over a certain Flock' (ibid., p. 513).

Those contemporaries who tamper with material drawn trom biblical sources never match the early Milton at his brightest, and most innovations are as slight as those cited from his 1649 tracts. Featley's introduction of the number of axe-strokes in 'This Heresie may be felled downe at three blowes of the axe' (*Dippers Dipt*, p. 129) produces a marginally more concrete image than its original, Matt. 3:10. The author of *Eikon Alethine* alters 'saying, Great is Diana of the Ephesians' (Acts 19:28) to 'to cry up his *Diana*' (p. 70). Again, in *Eikon Basilike* 'the little foxes, that spoil the vines' (Song 2:15) is expanded to '*subtil Foxes, to waste and deform Thy Vineyard*' (p. 145). The changes are rarely more interesting than these.

11. CONCLUSIONS

The comparison of Milton's first and final groups of tracts disclosed a radical shift in his prose style. The anti-prelatical tracts are luxuriant—rich in lexical variety and inventiveness and often leisurely in the development of their imagery—a sharp contrast with the spareness of the last pamphlets, which are characterized by a lexical sobriety and the use of fewer and terser images (though *Readie and Easie Way* shows some reversion to his earlier practice). Milton's procedure when adapting sacred material changes also towards a new reluctance to add to his sources and a greater tendency to quote and give references. His style becomes less adjectival, and he consistently favours postponing adjectives. A study of the intervenient tracts reveals the stages of this drastic transformation.

Milton's pamphlets of 1643 to 1645 are stylistically akin to his earlier tracts. He continues to use sets of synonyms in preference to repeating the same words for recurrent concepts. His neologizing has a playfulness, and he still indulges in unorthodox collocations. However, he begins to experiment with image density, using less imagery in works of plain exposition or close exegesis. Image structure, however, in general retains the character of the earlier tracts, expansive, and often with a strong narrative or dramatic quality.

The first major shift occurs in 1649. Milton retains his old habit of playing on sets of synonyms, and there remains a sparkle that distinguishes his neologizing from that of contemporaries, but unusual collocations become much less prominent, the image density falls to that of his last tracts, and his imagery loses the luxuriance that characterizes it earlier.

To complete the transformation to the style of the last tracts, it remained only for Milton to abandon the use of synonyms and the remaining features of lexical flamboyance, to use fewer adjectives, to employ more frequently adjectival postponement, and to adopt his careful policy of transmitting sacred material accurately and with acknowledgement when adapting imagery from biblical sources. Step by step Milton dismantled what was possibly the most exhilarating and inventive prose style of the seventeenth century and replaced it with a spare functionalism.

In the past there has been too much readiness to make asser-
tions about Milton's style without proper reference to the norms
of mid-century pamphlet-writing. To avoid this weakness, the
present study subjected a number of tracts by Milton's contemporaries (eighteen by fifteen writers) to the same tests used for
Milton's prose. From this exercise important facts have
emerged. A number of features which had previously been
claimed as characteristic of Milton must now be seen merely as
characteristic of mid-century controversial prose in general. At
the same time, we can isolate a number of features which are
genuinely Miltonic. Furthermore, Milton's own development
cannot be seen simply as a reflection of broader developments in
contemporary prose.

Nor can the development be explained away in terms of failing
artistic ability. In all probability, his final and most limited
tracts, except for *Of True Religion*, date from the period in which
he was writing *Paradise Lost*. There is no reason to suppose
Milton was incapable of continuing in his earliest prose style had
he so wished.

The reasons for the changes in Milton's style must remain the
subject of conjecture and hypothesis. I incline towards viewing
the development as a result of Milton's changing opinion of the
form appropriate for political literature. In the period from 1641
to 1645 the political pamphlet may have seemed to Milton to
present an opportunity for the exercise of a wide range of his
talents, in particular for the exhibition of his capacity for bril-
liantly inventive and unorthodox prose. By 1649—perhaps
because of the issues raised by the trial of the king; perhaps
because of his acceptance of paid employment under the Commonwealth government; perhaps because of an increased
melancholy, occasioned by his failing eyesight; perhaps because
of a new perception that the mass of the people were out of sympathy with the causes he championed—politics and political
writing assumed for Milton a deadly seriousness. He
refashioned his prose to meet new criteria of clarity and precision. Further changes in his last tracts completed the
process, leaving a prose style which is, if still eloquent, less
unorthodox and more ordinary. Yet the change should probably
be regarded not so much as a falling off as a growing up. The

anti-prelatical tracts exhibit an innocence, a certain naïvety, in the tacit assumption that brilliant style is what is needed in polemic, as if that in itself will be instrumental in swaying political opinion. It seems a maturer Milton who checks his exuberance and restricts himself to a more functional prose. He appears to recognize the relative powerlessness of the creative writer to influence events through the application of his art. The cooler medium of his 1649 tracts and more especially of his final pamphlets is the prose of a sadder but wiser man who has come to recognize the limitations of creative and unorthodox prose in shaping the crisis in which he finds himself.

Seventeenth-century prose largely remains critically unexplored, and surer interpretation of the significance of Milton's development is not feasible until we know much more about mid-century political writing. It is relatively easy for theoreticians to postulate dialectical relationships between literature and the socio-economic infrastructure. It is much more difficult to chart with precision the interaction between even such committed writing as seventeenth-century polemic and the developing crisis. Much more information is needed before we can attempt a higher synthesis. We have no accurate stylistic account of even such major writers as Gerrard Winstanley or Thomas Browne. The political pamphlet was quite a new and rapidly developing form, but our genre-history is so deficient that neither its antecedents nor its formal characteristics have been investigated. There seems to be very little known about the circumstances of pamphlet production. How were the tracts funded? Who could afford them? How were they distributed? How narrowly was their readership defined? Could the writer accurately predict who his readers would be? How strong a notion of 'target reader' did he entertain? The important concept of polemical strategy—the ways in which writers prompted and manipulated their readers' responses to achieve definable political objectives—remains completely unexplored. The questions are myriad, the answers, all of which could well influence our interpretation of Milton's prose, remain to be found.

APPENDIX[1]

The selection of texts for comparison with Milton's anti-prelatical tracts posed little problem. Milton's pamphlets were largely a contribution to a distinct controversy, the Smectymnuan debate, within the broader discussion about Church government. It was initiated by Joseph Hall's *Humble Remonstrance*, which Smectymnuus (an acronym from the names of its co-authors, Stephen Marshall, Edmund Calamy, Thomas Young, Matthew Newcomen, and William Spurstow) attacked in their *Answer to the Humble Remonstrance*. This provoked Hall's *Defence of the Humble Remonstrance*, which was in turn answered by Smectymnuus in their *Vindication of the Answer* and by Milton in *Animadversions*. Hall replied to the Smectymnuans in his *Short Answer* and an anonymous writer—probably Hall's son, perhaps in collaboration with his father[2]—replied to Milton in *A Modest Confutation*. The latter was answered by Milton in his *Apology*. The non-Miltonic tracts in this protracted exchange constitute a neatly defined group for comparison. The prelatical position assumed by Hall was supported by the publication of *Certain Briefe Treatises* (1641), a collection of moderate essays by Archbishop Ussher and other respected divines. This was a primary target of Milton's *Church-Government*. However, I decided not to use it for purposes of comparison because it is an anthology of brief pieces by several authors presenting no stylistic homogeneity and because some of the constituent tracts are markedly earlier.

No such cohesive group presented itself for comparison with Milton's tracts of 1643 to 1645 and selection was consequently more difficult. As representatives of radical opinion I opted for *The Bloudy Tenent of Persecution* by Roger Williams and *Mans Mortallitie* by 'R.O.', usually thought to be Richard Overton the Leveller.[3] The former as an attempt to remove boundaries to toleration is loosely an analogue to *Areopagitica*. Both were commonly bracketed with Milton's most notorious tract to date, *Doctrine and Discipline*, by more moderate puritans seeking to demonstrate the libertine excesses of the radical press, as in Pagitt's observation that

They preach, print and practise their hereticall opinions openly: for books, *vide* the bloody Tenet, witnesse the tractate of divorce in which the bonds are let loose to inordinate lust: a pamphlet also, in which the soul is laid asleepe from the house of judgement, with many others.[4]

The books all recur as objects of attack in, for example, *A Testimony to the Truth of Jesus Christ* (1648) by the Sion College Ministers[5] and in the anonymous broadsheet *These Tradesmen are Preachers* (1647). I took from the enemies of the sectaries the anonymous reply to Milton's first divorce tract, *An Answer to a Book, Intituled, The Doctrine and Discipline*, and one of the longer and more polished attacks on the sectaries, Daniel Featley's *Dippers Dipt*, primarily an anti-Baptist attack, which does, however, criticize Milton in passing (sig. B2v).

From the controversies about the deposition and execution of the King two pamphlets seemed particularly appropriate for comparison with Milton's—*Eikon Basilike*, ostensibly Charles's own apology and Milton's target in *Eikonoklastes*, and an anonymous attack on *Eikon Basilike*, *Eikon Alethine*. To these I added the royalist *Humble Address* by Henry Hammond, a royal chaplain. Milton possibly alludes to this tract in *Tenure* (III, 195 n. 26). From the republican apologies I chose John Canne's *Golden Rule*, a treatise apparently influenced by *Tenure*.[6]

The choice of texts for comparison with Milton's final tracts posed some difficulties. *Civil Power* and *Hirelings* were provoked by no tracts in particular, nor did they in turn attract any replies. The target of *Brief Notes*, Matthew Griffith's sermon, *The Fear of God and the King* (1660), was excluded from stylistic comparison because its origins were in oral delivery. I excluded several replies to Milton's other late tracts, also on generic grounds. The anonymous *Censure of the Rota* (1660), an attack on Milton feignedly emanating from the Rota Club, is a literary spoof, and as such belongs more properly to the genre of satirical parody. Again, *The Character of the Rump* (1660), also anonymous, and Sir Roger L'Estrange's *Be Merry and Wise* (1660), an answer to *Readie and Easie Way*, and his *No Blinde Guides* (1660), an answer to *Brief Notes*, were too brief to afford good material for comparison and the first two at least are more exercises in scurrilous lampoon than examples of serious prose.

However, I did choose one answer to *Readine and Easie Way, Dignity of Kingship* by 'G.S.', identified by William Riley Parker as George Starkey.[7] I added, as a representative of conservative Presbyterian opinion, William Prynne's *Brief Necessary Vindication*. Henry Stubbe's refreshingly undogmatic *Good Old Cause* presented an interesting analogue to Milton's *Civil Power*. From the final, desperate republican tracts I selected the ingenious *Interest Will Not Lie* by Marchemont Nedham, who was generally associated with Milton in the minds of contemporaries.[8]

NOTES

INTRODUCTION

1. See, e.g. Charles E. Osgood, 'Some Effects of Motivation', in *Style and Language*, ed. Thomas Sebeok (Cambridge, Mass. and New York, 1960), pp. 293-306, M. A. K. Halliday, Angus McIntosh, and Peter Strevens, *The Linguistic Sciences and Language Teaching* (1964), pp. 75-110, and D. Davy and D. Crystal, *Investigating English Style* (1969).
2. K. G. Hamilton, 'The Structure of Milton's Prose', in *Language and Style in Milton: A Symposium in Honor of the Tercentenary of "Paradise Lost"*, ed. R. D. Emma and J. T. Shawcross (New York, 1967), pp. 304-32.
3. Keith W. Stavely, *The Politics of Milton's Prose Style* (New Haven, 1975).
4. R. D. Emma, *Milton's Grammar* (The Hague, 1964).
5. For an account of the texts I selected and their relationship to Milton's writing see Appendix, below, p. 104.

CHAPTER 1

1. This is sometimes termed the 'token-type distinction'.
2. The computing was done at the Oxford University Computing Laboratory, supplemented by work run at the University of Manchester Regional Computing Centre, accessed through the University College of North Wales Computing Laboratory. I used the COCOA program. For a full account of its scope and application, see Godelieve L. M. Berry-Rogghe and T. D. Crawford, *COCOA Manual* (Didcot and Cardiff, 1973).

CHAPTER 2

1. I took many valuable suggestions for this and the corresponding chapter in Sect. 2 from C. J. E. Ball, 'Lexis: The Vocabulary of English', in *The English Language*, ed. W. F. Bolton (1975), pp. 214-45. Ball defines the useful notion of the 'core' of the language as 'the common stock of words which are neither literary nor colloquial, neither foreign nor dialectal, neither novel nor obsolescent, neither scientific nor technical' (p. 214).
2. I noted no significant distinction in these aspects of lexis between the two editions of *Readie and Easie Way*. All references in this chapter are to the 2nd edn.
3. Milton discusses the word in *Areopagitica* (II, 504-5), quoted and considered below, p. 70.
4. Lists of words coined by Milton and his contemporaries and of words used by them in new significations can be found in an appendix to my 'Studies in the Development of Milton's Prose Style', Oxford D. Phil. diss. (1977), pp. 246-60.

5. It shares certain characteristics with 'rose-red' ('red as a rose is red'), 'key-cold' ('cold as a key is cold'), etc., but clearly differs in being a noun-participle, not a noun-adjective compound. Again, its distribution resembles 'clay-moulded' or 'wood-built', but these merely mean 'moulded from clay' or 'built from wood', and are not exact analogues.

6. The form 'madamoisella' is interesting. I have found no evidence of the word having an '-a' termination in French (see *Dictionnaire de la langue française*, ed. E. Littré (Paris, 1881-3) and *Dictionnaire alphabétique et analogique de la langue française*, ed. P. Robert (Paris, 1958-64), s.v. 'Madamoiselle'), though the form was current in Italian (see *Grande Dizionario della Lingua Italiana*, ed. Salvatore Battaglia (Turin, 1961-), s.v. 'Madamigèlla'). Milton may consciously be borrowing from Italian to suggest a Mediterranean depravity or to point up further the alienism of the word.

7. F. E. Ekfelt, 'Latinate Diction in Milton's Prose', *PQ*, xxviii (1949), 53-71.

8. Noted by J. H. Neumann, 'Milton's Prose Vocabulary', PMLA, lx (1945), 108 n. 6.

9. *OED*, s.v. 'Decent', 1; 'Mediocrity', 2.

10. *OED*, s.v. 'Prevent', 3. This sense had been current since the early 16th century. Cp. Milton's 'O run, prevent them with thy humble ode', 'On the Morning of Christ's Nativity', l. 24, *Poems*, p. 102, as the Yale editor notes.

11. *OED*, s.v. 'Fume', sb., 1 b.

12. *OED*, s.v. 'Epicure', 2; 'Epicurean', sb., 2.

13. *OED*, s.v. 'Sconce', vb.^{2}, 1.

14. F. E. Ekfelt, 'The Graphic Diction of Milton's English Prose', *PQ*, xxv (1946), 54.

15. Hugh Sykes Davies, 'Milton and the Vocabulary of Verse and Prose', in *Literary English since Shakespeare*, ed. George Watson (New York, 1970), pp. 175-93.

16. Eric Partridge, *Slang Today and Yesterday*, 4th edn. (1970), p. 11.

17. This may well be an allusion to the legend that Alexander the Great, seeing Diogenes sunbathing, asked him what he could do for him, and received the answer, 'Don't keep the sun off me' ('Alexander', *Plutarch's Lives*, Loeb edn., (1914-26), vii, 258-9). Milton perhaps refers to the incident to suggest his own honourable rejection of preferment through patronage by the ecclesiastical hierarchy.

18. David Masson, *The Life of John Milton* (1859-94), ii, 261. For an account of how Milton's contemporaries may have viewed this aspect of his style, see my 'Obscenity, Slang and Indecorum in Milton's English Prose', *Prose Studies*, iii (1980), 5-14.

19. A. F. Price, 'Incidental Imagery in *Areopagitica*', *MP*, xlix (1952), 217-22, and J. X. Evans, 'Imagery as Argument in Milton's *Areopagitica*', *Texas Studies in Literature and Language*, viii (1966), 189-205.

20. *OED*, s.v. 'Spend', vb., 9 b.

CHAPTER 3

1. Considered above, p.xi.
2. See Fowler's comments in Milton, *Poems*, pp. 429-30.
3. He uses *Animadversions, Church-Government, Areopagitica*, and *Tenure*.
4. L. T. Milic, *A Quantitative Approach to the Style of Jonathan Swift* (The Hague, 1967), pp. 144-8. His system is adapted from that developed by C. C. Fries in his *Structure of English* (1952: rpt. 1957).
5. Certainly a later suggestion (that the low incidence of verbs which he notes is a consequence of high incidence of adjectives (p. 86)) is meant to apply to the prose as well as the poetry.
6. See above, p. 5 and below, p. 44.
7. Emma's findings on this point are difficult to interpret because, in the case of Eliot and Shakespeare, he does not distinguish between participles and other verbal forms which share the '-ed' and '-ing' inflections (pp. 107-9).

CHAPTER 4

1. Op. cit.
2. Op. cit.
3. He uses the same samples on which he bases his observations of other aspects of Miltonic grammar.
4. Op. cit., p. 307.
5. Ibid., p. 331.
6. Ibid., p. 306.
7. I have adopted Emma's practice of repunctuating Milton's text along modern, logical and syntactical lines. There is ample evidence that the punctuation represents the inconsistent interaction of Milton's own old-fashioned and rhetorical practice and the more modern, logical punctuation of the printing-shops (see Mindele Treip, *Milton's Punctuation and Changing English Usage 1582-1676* (1970), *passim*, and my 'Punctuation in Milton's Vernacular Prose', *Notes and Queries*, n.s., xxv (1978), 18-19). I considered a unit of text to be a sentence if it was grammatically complete, could be terminated without leaving grammatically incomplete fragments in residue, and made good sense. I applied the same criteria in normalizing the non-Miltonic texts. Prynne poses some problems that cannot be thus resolved, since to some extent he organizes his pamphlets like legal documents, with numbered paragraphs which often contain grammatically independent material but which are grammatically dependent on earlier sentences. If they were taken with the sentences on which they depend they would constitute units of several hundred words and there would remain unresolved the problem of how to analyse the completely independent sentences the paragraphs contain. The best option seemed to be to regard these paragraphs as independent of what precedes them. Inevitably, a fairly strong element of subjectivity remains in the process of repunctuation. There is scope for disagreement about which division does indeed make the best sense. This approach, however, seems the best of the alternatives open. At least it focuses the analysis in a fairly consistent way on the writer's syntactical

predilection, and not on the whims and vagaries of his or his printer's punctuation.

8. L. P. Wilkinson, *Golden Latin Artistry* (Cambridge, 1963), p. 175.

9. Treip, op. cit., p. 23.

10. Op. cit., pp. 308-9.

11. Op. cit., esp. Ch. 1. He avoids formal definition, though it is fairly clear how he uses his terms.

12. Richard Ohmann, 'Generative Grammar and the Concept of Literary Style', *Word*, xx (1964), 423-39.

CHAPTER 5

1. Wolfgang Clemen, *Shakespeares Bilder: Ihre Entwicklung und ihre Funktionen im Dramatischen Werk*, Bonner Studien zur Englischen Philologie, Heft xxvii (Bonn, 1936); *The Development of Shakespeare's Imagery* (1951: rpt. 1967).

2. Christine Brooke-Rose, *A Grammar of Metaphor* (1958); 'Metaphor in *Paradise Lost*: a Grammatical Analysis', in Emma and Shawcross, op. cit., pp. 252-303.

3. See, e.g. Cicero, *De Oratore*, Loeb edn. (1942), ii, 121-3; Quintilian, *Institutio Oratoria*, Loeb edn. (1921-2), iii, 303.

4. Terence Hawkes, *Metaphor* (1972), p. 1.

5. *OED*, s.v. 'Boisterous', 3, 'Rough, massive, bulky, big and cumbrous'.

6. 'Obscurity' puns on *OED* 1, 'Absence of light (total or partial); darkness; dimness, dullness; *concr.* a dark place' and 2, 'The quality or condition of being unknown, inconspicuous, or insignificant'.

7. He calls himself 'a dutiful Sonne of the Church' on the title page of *Humble Remonstrance*.

8. e.g. in 'In your next Section, like ill-bred sonnes, you spit in the face of your Mother; a Mother too good for such sonnes, the Church of England . . .' (*Defence of the Humble Remonstrance*, p. 149).

9. The *OED* cites this s.v. 'Mummery' as an example of 2, 'Ridiculous ceremonial or "play-acting"; an instance of this. Often applied to religious ritual regarded as silly or hypocritical'. No doubt Milton did regard such ritual as mummery, but it is clear that here he is censuring not the bishops' sermon-acting, but their claim to expound exclusively the doctrines of the Church.

10. L. C. Knights, 'Bacon and the Seventeenth-century Dissociation of Sensibility', *Explorations* (1946: rpt. 1963), 92-111.

11. e.g. John Carey, *Milton* (1969), p. 68.

12. On Milton's use of this translation in preference to the others available to him see H. F. Fletcher, *The Use of the Bible in Milton's Vernacular Prose* (Urbana, 1929). Fletcher also notes a greater tendency to quote exactly from the Authorized Version in Milton's later tracts.

13. Erich Auerbach, *Mimesis*, trans. Willard R. Trask (1953: rpt. Princeton, 1968), p. 9.

14. *OED*, s.v. 'Rear', v[1].

15. See Leo Miller, *Explicator*, xxvi (Sept. 1967), Item 5, for an account of this passage.

16. *OED*, s.v. 'Vomit', sb., 4.

CHAPTER 7

1. See above, p. 1.
2. *OED*, s.v. 'Attorney', 3 and 'Solicitor', 3.
3. I am indebted to J. L. Barton of Merton College, Oxford, for clarification on this point.

CHAPTER 8

1. See above, p. 10.
2. In *Histrio-mastix* (1633), p. 701. 4.
3. I use No. 22 in F. F. Madan's *New Bibliography of the 'Eikon Basilike' of King Charles the First* (Oxford, 1950), on Madan's account the 1st edn. to contain the appendix of prayers.
4. *Eikon Aklastos* (n.p., 1651), pp. 115-6.
5. Thomas Hobbes, *Philosophicall Rudiments Concerning Government and Society* (1651), p. 153.
6. All references in this chapter are to the 2nd edn. of *Doctrine and Discipline*. In broad terms Milton's approach to the lexical aspects of style seems the same in both editions.
7. See above, pp.10-11.
8. *Life*, iii, 235.
9. For an abbreviated list see Yale, ii, 187.
10. *OED*, s.v. 'Minorite', 1 and 2.
11. *OED*, s.v. 'Ethic', B II 2 b.
12. *OED*, s.v. 'Gnome' and 'Etymology'.
13. The word is first recorded by the *OED* in 1715.
14. *OED*, s.v. 'Coaxation'.
15. Cf. the Lady's condemnation of Comus:
    Enjoy your dear wit, and gay rhetoric
    That hath so well been taught her dazzling fence,
    Thou art not fit to hear thyself convinced (*Comus*, ll. 789-91, *Poems*, p. 216.)
16. To the modern reader the word may seem an allusion to the phrase 'to bark one's shins'. This expression, however, is of much later origin. See *OED*, s.v. 'Bark', v^2., 3 b.
17. See above, p. 6.
18. *OED*, s.v. 'Sucking', 3 a.
19. See above, pp. 6-7.
20. e.g. imagery on pp. 226, 241, 254, 282-3.
21. See above, pp. 17-18.

CHAPTER 9

1. See above, p. 22.
2. See above, p. 24.

CHAPTER 10

1. See above, p. 45.
2. See above, p. 44.
3. W. R. Parker, *Milton* (Oxford, 1968), ii, 897.
4. Milton, Sonnet XII, 'On the Detraction which followed my writing Certain Treatises', ll. 1-7, *Poems*, pp. 294-5.
5. See Harris F. Fletcher, *The Intellectual Development of John Milton* (Urbana, 1956-), i, 221, 224-5, for an account of the teaching of rhetoric at St. Paul's School.
6. Sonnet XI, l. 2, *Poems*, p. 305.
7. See W. R. Parker, *Milton's Contemporary Reputation* (Columbus, 1940), pp. 17-19.
8. See above, p. 46.
9. The so-called Pamela controversy, about whether the apparent borrowing from Sidney was inserted into the *Eikon* by government agents, perhaps under the direction of Milton, seems ultimately resolved by Madan, op. cit., pp. 120-1. The issue is reviewed by M. Y. Hughes in Yale, iii, 152-9.
10. *OED*, s.v. 'Dialogue', 2 b.
11. Quoted above, p. 48.
12. See above, p. 90.
13. See above, p. 56.
14. See above, p. 57.
15. See above, pp. 58-9.
16. See above, pp. 60-2.

APPENDIX

1. Christopher Hill provides the fullest and most recent account of Milton's political milieu in his *Milton and the English Revolution* (1977). This, however, appeared too late to influence my selection of texts for comparison.
2. See Masson, *Life*, ii, 394.
3. For a review of the debate about this attribution see Harold Fisch's introduction to his *Mans Mortalitie* (Liverpool, 1968), pp. xii-xv.
4. Ephraim Pagitt, *Heresiography* (1645), sig. A3v.
5. The references to Milton are on p. 19, to *Bloudy Tenent*, on p. 22, to *Mans Mortallitie*, *passim*.
6. See George W. Whiting, *Milton's Literary Milieu* (Chapel Hill, 1939), pp. 311-23.
7. In the introduction to his edition of the text (New York, 1942), pp. x-xii.
8. L'Estrange called them a 'Couple of *Currs* of the same *Pack*' in *L'Estrange His Apology* (1660), p. 113; see also Henry Foulis, *The History of the Wicked Plots* (1662), p. 24 and Richard Leigh (attrib.), *The Transproser Rehears'd* (1673), p. 32.

BIBLIOGRAPHY

Unless otherwise stated, the place of publication is London. STC, Wing, or Madan numbers are given where plurality of editions of the same date and place of origin may make identification of the edition used difficult.

WORKS BY MILTON AND HIS CONTEMPORARIES

ANON., *An Answer to a Book, Intituled, The Doctrine and Discipline of Divorce*, 1644.

ANON., *The Censure of the Rota Upon Mr Miltons Book, Entituled Readie and Easie Way*, 1660.

ANON., *Eikon Alethine*, 1649.

ANON., *A Modest Confutation of a Slanderous and Scurrilous Libell, Entituled, Animadversions*, 1642.

ANON., *These Trades-men are Preachers in and about the City of London*, 1647.

CANNE, JOHN, *The Golden Rule, Or, Justice Advanced*, 1649.

CHARLES I, *Eikon Basilike*, 1649, Madan 22.

FEATLEY, DANIEL, *The Dippers Dipt*, 1645.

FOULIS, HENRY, *The History of the Wicked Plots and Conspiracies of Our Pretended Saints*, 1662.

GRIFFITH, MATTHEW, *The Fear of God and the King*, 1660.

HALL, JOSEPH, *A Defence of the Humble Remonstrance*, 1641.

—— *An Humble Remonstrance to the High Court of Parliament*, 1640, STC 12675.

—— *A Short Answer to the Tedious Vindication of Smectymnuus*, 1641.

HAMMOND, HENRY, *To the Right Honourable, the Lord Fairfax, and His Councell of Warre: The Humble Addresse*, 1649, Wing H 607.

HOBBES, THOMAS, *Philosophicall Rudiments Concerning Government and Society*, 1651.

JANE, JOSEPH, *Eikon Aklastos*, n. p., 1651.

LEIGH, RICHARD, *The Transproser Rehears'd: or, The Fifth Act of Mr. Bayes's Play*, Oxford, 1673.

L'ESTRANGE, SIR ROGER, *Be Merry and Wise*, 1660.

—— *L'Estrange His Apology*, 1660.

—— *No Blinde Guides, In Answer to a seditious Pamphlet of J. Miltons, Intituled Brief Notes*, 1660.

MILTON, JOHN, *Complete Prose Works of John Milton*, ed. Don M. Wolfe *et al.*, 8 vols., New Haven, 1953-.

—— *The Poems of John Milton*, ed. John Carey and Alastair Fowler, 1968.

—— *The Works of John Milton*, ed. Frank Allen Patterson *et al.*, 18 vols., New York, 1931-8.

NEDHAM, MARCHEMONT, *Interest Will Not Lie*, 1659.

O., R., *Mans Mortalitie*, ed. Harold Fisch, Liverpool, 1968.

—— *Mans Mortallitie*, Amsterdam, 1643.

PAGITT, EPHRAIM, *Heresiography: or, a Description of the Heretickes and Sectaries of the Latter Times*, 1645, Wing P 174.

PRYNNE, WILLIAM, *A Brief Necessary Vindication of the Old and New Secluded Members*, 1659, Wing P 3913.

—— *Histrio-Mastix*, 1633.

S., G., *The Dignity of Kingship Asserted*, 1660.

—— *The Dignity of Kingship Asserted*, ed. William Riley Parker, Publication No. 54 of the Facsimile Text Society, New York, 1942.

SION COLLEGE MINISTERS, *A Testimony to the Truth of Jesus Christ and to Our Solemn League and Covenant*, 1648.

SMECTYMNUUS, *An Answer to a Book Entitled, an Humble Remonstrance*, 1641, Wing M 748A.

—— *A Vindication of the Answer to the Humble Remonstrance*, 1641, Wing M 798.

STUBBE, HENRY *An Essay in Defence of the Good Old Cause*, 1659.

USSHER, JAMES *et al.*, *Certain Briefe Treatises*, 1641.

WILLIAMS, ROGER, *The Bloudy Tenent of Persecution for cause of Conscience*, 1644, Wing W 2758.

OTHER WORKS

AUERBACH, ERICH, *Mimesis*, trans. Willard Trask, 1953: rpt., Princeton, 1968.

BALL, C. J. E., 'Lexis: The Vocabulary of English', in *The English Language*, ed. Whitney F. Bolton, 1975, pp. 214-45.

BATTAGLIA, SALVATORE, *Grande Dizionario della Lingua Italiana*, Turin, 1961-.

CAREY, JOHN, *Milton*, 1968.

CICERO, *De Oratore*, Loeb Classical Library, 2 vols., 1942.

CLEMEN, WOLFGANG, *The Development of Shakespeare's Imagery*, 1951: rpt. 1967.

—— *Shakespeares Bilder: Ihre Entwicklung und Ihre Funktionen im Dramatischen Werk*, Bonner Studien zur Englischen Philologie, Heft xxvii, Bonn, 1936.

CORNS, THOMAS N., 'Punctuation in Milton's Vernacular Prose', *Notes and Queries*, n. s., xxv (1978), 18-19.

——— 'Obscenity, Slang and Indecorum in Milton's English Prose', *Prose Studies*, iii (1980), 5-14.

——— 'Studies in the Development of Milton's Prose Style', Oxford D. Phil. diss., 1977.

DAVIES, HUGH SYKES, 'Milton and the Vocabulary of Verse and Prose', in *Literary English Since Shakespeare*, ed. George Watson, New York, 1970, pp. 175-93.

DAVY, D., and CRYSTAL, D., *Investigating English Style*, 1969.

EKFELT, FRED EMIL, 'The Graphic Diction in Milton's English Prose', *PQ* xxv (1946), 46-69.

——— 'Latinate Diction in Milton's English Prose', *PQ* xxviii (1949), 53-71.

EMMA, RONALD DAVID, *Milton's Grammar*, The Hague, 1964.

——— and SHAWCROSS, JOHN T. (eds.), *Language and Style in Milton*, A Symposium in Honor of the Tercentenary of *Paradise Lost*, New York, 1967.

EVANS, JOHN X., 'Imagery as Argument in Milton'a *Areopagitica*', *Texas Studies in Literature and Language*, viii (1966), 189-215.

FLETCHER, HARRIS FRANCIS, *The Intellectual Development of John Milton*, Urbana, 1956-.

——— *The Use of the Bible in Milton's Vernacular Prose*, Urbana, 1929.

FRIES, C. C., *The Structure of English*, 1952: rpt. 1957.

HALLIDAY, M. A. K., MCINTOSH, ANGUS, and STREVENS, PETER, *The Linguistic Sciences and Language Teaching*, 1964.

HAMILTON, K. G., 'The Structure of Milton's Prose', in *Language and Style in Milton*, ed. Emma and Shawcross, New York, 1967, pp. 304-32.

HAWKES, TERENCE, *Metaphor*, The Critical Idiom, No. 25, 1972.

HILL, CHRISTOPHER, *Milton and the English Revolution*, 1977.

KNIGHTS, L. C., 'Bacon and the Seventeenth-century Dissociation of Sensibility', in his *Explorations*, 1946: rpt. 1963, pp. 92-111.

LITTRÉ, E. (ed.), *Dictionnaire de la langue française*, Paris, 1881-3.

MADAN, F. F., *A New Bibliography of the 'Eikon Basilike' of King Charles the First with a note on the Authorship*, Oxford Bibliographical Society Publications, n.s., iii (1949), Oxford, 1950.

MASSON, DAVID, *The Life of John Milton*, 7 vols., 1859-94.

MILIC, LOIUS TONKO, *A Quantitative Approach to the Style of Jonathan Swift*, The Hague, 1967.

MILLER, LEO, Item 5, *Explicator*, xxvi (Sept. 1967).

NEUMANN, JOSHUA H., 'Milton's Prose Vocabulary', *PMLA*, lx (1945), 102-20.

OHMANN, RICHARD, 'Generative Grammar and the Concept of Literary Style', *Word*, xx (1964), 423-39, rpt. in *Readings in Applied*

Transformational Grammar, ed. Mark Lester, New York, 1970, pp. 117-36.

OSGOOD, CHARLES E., 'Some Effects of Motivation', in *Style and Language*, ed. Thomas Sebeok, Cambridge, Mass. and New York, 1960, pp. 293-306.

PARKER, WILLIAM RILEY, *Milton: A Biography*, 2 vols., Oxford, 1968.

—— *Milton's Contemporary Reputation*, Columbus, Ohio, 1940.

PARTRIDGE, ERIC, *Slang Today and Yesterday*, 4th edn., 1970.

PLUTARCH, *Lives*. Loeb Classical Library, 11 vols., 1914-26.

PRICE, ALAN F., 'Incidental Imagery in *Areopagitica*', *MP*, xlix (1952), 217-22.

QUINTILIAN, *The Institutio Oratoria*, Loeb Classical Library, 4 vols., 1921-2.

ROBERT, P., *Dictionnaire alphabétique et analogique de la langue française*, Paris, 1958-64.

ROGGHE, GODELIEVE L. M. BERRY- and CRAWFORD, T. D., *COCOA Manual*, Didcot and Cardiff, 1973.

ROSE, CHRISTINE BROOKE-, *A Grammar of Metaphor*, 1958.

—— 'Metaphor in *Paradise Lost*: a Grammatical Analysis', in *Language and Style in Milton*, ed. Emma and Shawcross, pp. 252-303.

STAVELY, KEITH W., *The Politics of Milton's Prose Style*, New Haven, 1975.

TREIP, MINDELE, *Milton's Punctuation and Changing English Usage, 1582-1676*, 1970.

WHITING, GEORGE W., *Milton's Literary Milieu*, Chapel Hill, 1939.

WILKINSON, L. P., *Golden Latin Artistry*, Cambridge, 1963.

INDEX

Answer to a Book 67, 68, 77, 105
Aristophanes 73
Aristotle 72
Auerbach, Erich 60

Bacon, Sir Francis 50
Ball, C. J. E. 106
Browne, Sir Thomas xi, 103

Canne, John 75, 77, 95, 96, 105
Censure of the Rota 105
Charles I, *Eikon Basilike* 69, 73, 75, 76,
    77, 78, 90, 95, 100, 105
Cicero 109
Clemen, Wolfgang 43
COCOA 21
Comenius, John Amos 71

Davies, Hugh Sykes 14

Eikon Alethine 70, 73, 75, 77, 88, 95, 96,
    105
Eikon Basilike, see Charles I.
Ekfelt, Fred E. 14
Eliot, T. S. xi, 20
Emma, Ronald D. 20ff, 31, 35
Evans, John X. 109

Featley, Daniel 73, 75, 77, 78, 95, 100,
    105
Fletcher, Harris F. 109
Foulis, Henry 114

Griffith, Matthew 105

Hall, Joseph, *Defence of Humble
    Remonstrance* 6, 8, 11, 18, 104; *Humble
    Remonstrance* 11, 18, 104; *Short Answer*
    6, 32, 50, 54, 104
Hamilton, K. G. xi, 31, 35
Hammond, Henry 76, 105
Hartlib, Samuel 71
Hawkes, Terence 43
Hill, Christopher 111
Hobbes, Thomas 70
Hooker, Richard xi

Jane, Joseph 69f

Knights, L. C. 50

Leigh, Richard 111
L'Estrange, Sir Roger 105
Levellers xi

Madan, F. F. 110
Masson, David 15, 71
Milic, Louis T. 21
Milton, John, *Animadversions* 6, 7, 9, 10,
    13, 14, 15, 17, 18, 34, 49, 51, 52, 53,
    57; *Apology* 3, 9, 10, 11, 12, 13, 14,
    16, 17, 18, 32, 39, 50, 57; *Areopagitica*
    70, 71, 72, 73, 74, 76, 78, 79, 84, 91,
    93, 97, 99; *Brief Notes* 3, 10; *Church--
    Government* 4, 9, 10, 11, 12, 16, 17, 25,
    49, 55, 57, 58, 61, 62, 90; *Civil Power*
    3, 40, 47; *Colasterion* 67, 68, 69, 74, 77,
    78; *Comus* 110; *Doctrine* 67, 73, 74, 76,
    77, 78, 84, 86, 89, 91, 96, 97, 99;
    Eikonoklastes 67, 69, 72, 74, 75, 76, 77,
    78, 79, 90, 93, 94, 96, 97, 99, 100;
    Hirelings 6, 8, 9, 10, 13, 14, 24, 25, 47,
    52, 59, 62; *Observations* 67, 74, 76, 77,
    96; *Of Education* 67, 71, 72, 92; *Of
    Reformation* 6, 7, 9, 10, 13, 15, 16, 18,
    46, 47, 48, 49, 50, 53, 61, 62, 94; *Of
    True Religion* 4, 9, 10, 58; *Prelatical
    Episcopacy* 4, 6, 7, 9, 14, 17, 24, 41, 49;
    Readie and Easie Way 6, 8, 15, 17, 25,
    28, 47, 50, 52, 62; *Sonnet XI* 85;
    Sonnet XII, 'On the Detraction which
    followed my writing Certain Treatises'
    84; *Tenure* 74, 76, 78; *Tetrachordon* 72,
    73, 74, 75, 76, 77, 78, 93, 96
Modest Confutation 18, 32, 104

Nedham, Marchemont 8, 15, 51, 52, 105
Neumann, Joshua H. 107

O., R., 78, 96, 104
Ohmann, Richard 35
Ormond, Marquis of 87

Pagitt, Ephraim 104
Parker, William R. 84, 111
Partridge, Eric 14
Plutarch 107
Price, Alan F. 107
Prynne, William, *Brief Necessary
    Vindication* 6, 11, 52, 105; *Histrio-
    Mastix* 110

Quintilian 109

Rose, Christine Brooke- 43

S., G. 7, 8, 11, 19, 51, 52, 54, 63, 105
Shakespeare, William xi, 20
Sidney, Sir Philip 72
Sion College Minister 105
Sirluck, Ernest 71
Smectymnuus, *Answer to Humble
    Remonstrance* 6, 8, 51, 52, 104;
    Vindication of Answer 11, 12, 54, 104

Stavely, Keith W., xi, 31, 35
Stubbe, Henry 11, 51, 52, 105

Treip, Mindele 108

Ussher, James 104

Winstanley, Gerrard 103